For Naomi and Zoe

The Great Aussie Bloke's Cookbook

Kim Terakes

Photography by Rob Palmer

VIKING
an imprint of
PENGUIN BOOKS

Contents

USBAND SON TEAM-MATE GRAN
OYFRIEND GRANDSON UNCLE FAT
 SON TEAM-MATE GRANDPA LOV
EMATE BOYFRIEND GRANDSON U
USBAND SON TEAM-MATE GRAN
ROTHER HOUSEMATE BOYFRIEND
LE FATHER HUSBAND SON TEAM-
 LOVER BROTHER HOUSEMATE B
RANDSON UNCLE FATHER HUSBA
NDPA LOVER BROTHER HOUSE-

About me

'I'm not a chef, I'm just a bloke who cooks a bit.'

With my daughter, Zoe.
The hats are the wrong way around.

Let me introduce myself. And get me out of the way.

I'm a bloke (a fifty-year-old, big, fat, balding bloke), and I can cook. I'm not a chef, I'm not trained, but I can cook a bit. I'm not really sure why. I grew up the eldest of three boys in a nice middle-class Sydney family in the sixties. Dad worked hard, Mum stayed at home and did all the cooking, though Dad would chip in now and then as well. They cooked the food of the day: bland English stuff. Grey meat and a portfolio of seven vegetables, all overcooked to buggery. Dad is a second-generation, full-blooded Greek, who somehow doesn't eat garlic and makes a moussaka that tastes like cardboard. Mum was forever baking cakes, and throughout my teens our house was always full of my hungry mates, which may be where my sense of hospitality comes from. My parents had a lot of Chinese friends, and Sunday-night Chinese, either in a modest restaurant in Chinatown or takeaway, was my weekly culinary treat. Even as a tot, I remember obsessing about it – just the start of a lifetime's obsession with food.

My other fixation is rugby. My rugby career, if that's what you could call it, lasted nearly 300 games all up, until I was thirty-seven years old. At the end, I was seventeen-stone-four in the old money, still playing five-eight and, as always, captain. (I figured out very early on that if you were captain, or better still, captain-coach, you got to pick your own position – never play in a single-digit jersey was my motto.) So I captain-coached at Macquarie Uni from the age of eighteen, and wound up as captain of Melbourne's Gerries (geriatrics) in my mid-thirties, only two games after I arrived, because the other players found it easier than trying to shut me up. I was a terrible footballer (I never played a game in first-grade in all those years) but I loved it, and even managed to combine it with my passion for food. Back when I was still a teenager I would cook an appalling chicken casserole, dubbed 'Chicken Terakes', for a hundred or so people after the game and somehow became 'BBQ consultant' as well, because I was the only one who could cook onions without burning them.

As well as my culinary exploits at the footy club, I've been an enthusiastic cook ever since I left home, often entertaining friends with slap-up dinners of up to a dozen courses (they thought I was certifiably mad – and they were probably right). Years ago, I combined my cooking skills with my abject sleaziness to persuade my future-wife Naomi and her friends to wear lingerie to dinner in exchange for a meal, the first of what became known as the 'no look, no cook' dinners. A career in advertising meant I ate lunch in a restaurant virtually every working day since the age of twenty-two, and my cooking kept improving as I ate out more and more, and took myself off to a few cooking classes. But the turning point for me, food-wise, came when I was organising an advertorial for *Australian Gourmet Traveller* magazine back in the late eighties. The editor, Karen Hammial, asked me if I could take some photos in Tuscany for the piece while I was on holidays. I happily agreed, and in one of those seemed-like-nothing-much-at-the-time-but-turned-out-to-be-life-changing moments, I sent her the itinerary for my five-week European jaunt, which included lunch and dinner out every day, with a total tally of about thirty Michelin stars. 'Terakes, you're a nut-case,' she boomed down the phone at me later. 'What do you do on your holidays, take photos in cake shops?' 'Well, yes,' was my sensible reply. (To this day, my idea of a holiday is going to France, eating every meal out, and filling the time in between hanging around markets and food stores.) So she asked me to write an article while I was there and, incapable as I am of writing to length, I wrote enough for five articles, and Karen ran them all. This kick-started my food-writing career, and for the past twenty years I've been combining my love of food with my deft ability to rabbit on about it. I've written for the likes of the *Sun-Herald*, *Vogue Entertaining* and *GQ*, among others and, along the way, I've been lucky enough to talk to many great chefs, restaurateurs and provedores who live their lives in the pursuit of good food.

The inspiration for my Boys Can Cook cooking classes

(boyscancook.com.au) came from writing for a predominantly male audience at *GQ*. I realised that many blokes were keen to learn the basics of cooking, but it had to be in the right environment – no stuffy 'masterclasses' would work for them. So, in 2004 I started classes for blokes that would arm them with some basic cooking knowledge while they watched the sport on TV, had a few drinks and hopefully a few laughs along the way. It proved a pretty successful formula, and soon the classes began to book out. This led to the establishment of my barbecue business, aussiebarbie.com.au, which began in 2006 and celebrates all things barbie.

These cooking classes have been a revelation to me. Many of those who attend lack even the most basic knowledge of food and cooking, yet it is really gratifying how willing they are to learn. I get a huge sense of satisfaction when guys report back after a class, having successfully cooked a meal for the first time. Or hearing guys in their early twenties (whose mums paid for the classes so their sons wouldn't starve), planning what they're going to cook for their girlfriends. I even had one guy's wife ring me in tears at nine o'clock on a Sunday night to thank me – her husband had just cooked his first meal in however-many years of marriage. While the classes are primarily for boys, I'm constantly surprised at the number of girls who attend (despite the odd tongue-in-cheek comment like the one made by an old rugby player at our first-ever class after one of the girls went to the toilet: 'Someone left the toilet seat down. Manners cost nothing, you know.') That said, the mood is decidedly inclusive, and the classes are now as much a social event as they are an educational one. We have regulars who come nearly every week. There have been romances (well, sex) and plenty of friendships have been forged. And the feedback has been telling – one enthusiastic semi-regular swears by the raspberry soufflé from my Food to Seduce class, reporting a perfect strike-rate with it.

Happily, my life is now 100 per cent food. As well as the cooking school and the barbecue business, I consult to major food marketers, shopping centres and restaurants, as well as predicting future food trends. And, I still do all the cooking at home – my wife has not cooked a meal for twenty-five years, and our daughter, Zoe, is under the impression that everyone's dad makes sushi on a school night. So, bad rugby, advertising lunches, eating my way around France, writing food columns, twelve courses for my mates then breakfast, lunch and dinner for my wife and daughter – it's a funny old life, but hopefully this helps to give you a sense of where the recipes and advice in *The Great Aussie Bloke's Cookbook* have come from.

Straight off the footy field and into a soufflé! (from *Australian Gourmet Traveller*, 1989)

At my happiest: eating myself to a standstill in France.

Throwing together four or five dishes, watching sport on TV and having a few laughs in one of my Boys Can Cook classes.

About the book

Boys can cook. Of course we can. It's only a matter of wanting to. If I can cook, anyone can.

Despite the fact that most of the world's great chefs are blokes, a lot of men still think that cooking is 'women's work'. Bollocks. This may have been true in the days when Fred came home from a hard day at the rockpile to find that Wilma had the cave cleaned, the kids bathed and dinner on the table. These days, there's probably no Wilma until Fred's in his early thirties. And when he does settle down with her, she'll most likely have a bigger job than he has and not much interest in cooking his dinner. Plus, there's a good chance Wilma will run off with Barney (or Betty), and leave Fred with a kitchen that has no set of instructions. So, as the world changes, we fellas not only *need* to cook more, but we should also *want* to cook more. Mostly, because it's fun. Cooking is relaxing; it's an escape from our own personal rockpiles. It gives you a sense of satisfaction – you achieve something every time you cook. But most importantly, cooking is about sharing something special with the people you care about. Whether you're cooking dinner for the kids, rustling up a flash dinner party or just something to wolf down in front of the footy with the boys, cooking demonstrates a generosity of spirit that is heartwarmingly rewarding.

Our lives are made up of many chapters: young and single, shacked up (probably), married (maybe), kids (possibly), divorced (quite likely), retired (hopefully). Whatever stage of life you're at, I hope this book will provide plenty of useful ideas. It isn't for those people who are already accomplished cooks – they should be off reading books by the likes of Tetsuya, Neil Perry and David Thompson. It's for those who are intimidated by such serious tomes, and even the whole idea of cooking. You won't become a Michelin-starred chef by using this book, but you will be able to produce a heap of simple, flavoursome dishes, and hopefully enjoy yourself while you're at it.

This book is a compilation of the most popular recipes from my cooking classes, a few of which are my interpre-tations of dishes I've enjoyed in restaurants or found in magazines and cookbooks over the years, and that I've adapted along the way to suit my own tastes. Some of the recipes here are contemporary, some are classics, and some are magnificently and unashamedly daggy. And though they are grouped by occasion, you should feel free to mix things up a bit. Some of the 'School-night staples' would fit well at a casual dinner party, and the 'Leaving home' recipes would suit most occasions, though I wouldn't suggest swapping any of the recipes from 'Food to seduce' with 'Food to watch the footy with' – things could get ugly.

You'll find some general hints at the front of the book and other advice throughout, which will help you get better results from your cooking, and maybe save you time. These nuggets of information are the results of the thousands of mistakes that I have made on your behalf over the past twenty-five years – everything from buying baking dishes too big to fit into my oven to forgetting to serve an entire course at a dinner party (blame the demon drink).

Now, don't be a cat and dog it, as we used to say when playing footy. You've come this far, you've got the book in your hand, so you might as well use it. I didn't write it for you to flick through and find recipes you like the look of and then ask your wife or girlfriend or boyfriend to cook them for you. I want you to experience the pleasure of finding a recipe or two, shopping for great ingredients, putting it all together and serving a meal to friends or family. Not food for survival, but food for pleasure – theirs and yours. What's the worst that can happen? You screw it up. Big deal. Screwed-up real food will probably still be better than the stuff you get from a fast-food joint or out of a can.

Finally, just as we do in my cooking classes, I suggest you crack open your beverage of choice, manoeuvre the TV into your line of sight and watch some sport while you cook. Because it's what blokes do.

Enjoy your cooking.

Some things a bloke should know

Buying top quality produce is the most important lesson you can learn

The better the quality of the produce you start with, the less you'll have to do to it and the better the end result will be. Obvious, isn't it?

Global transportation, sophisticated farming techniques and the influence of the two major supermarket chains mean that most types of produce are available to us all year round. This may be convenient, but it's a great pity if it makes us too accepting of good-looking but dull-tasting produce with a long shelf life (the pale, flavourless asparagus imported from Thailand is a good example), instead of enjoying things when they're at their best. There's a simple joy to eating in-season produce that is absolutely fresh, and when the season comes to a close, then there's the delicious anticipation of waiting until next year.

Learn to shop

To find out about seasonality and where to buy the best fresh produce, try talking to friends who are good cooks, or reading the foodie magazines and newspaper supplements. Then get out there and have a go – only experience can tell you how soft a ripe fig or avocado should feel, what prawns that have been frozen look like, or how heavy a nice flesh-filled crab should be.

Strike up a conversation with your butcher, greengrocer or fishmonger and ask them for their advice and recommendations. A good retailer who is passionate about their produce should be happy to help you. Buy your meat from independent butchers, where you can have this kind of dialogue, rather than one-stop shops like supermarkets. Ham sliced off the bone from a good butcher has miles more flavour than those tissue-thin slices you get in little plastic packs. Try specialty meat brands such as Barossa Chooks, White Rocks veal, Illabo lamb and Bangalow pork, or explore the grades of Wagyu beef – it'll be more expensive than your average stuff, but they don't say 'you get what you pay for' for nothing.

As a rule, try to avoid anything frozen (other than ice cream, puff pastry and maybe frozen peas on school nights). I want to shake people by the shoulders when I see their supermarket trolleys stacked high with frozen vegetables as they walk straight past the fresh ones. And it's fun to experiment with 'exotic' ingredients. For example, you won't believe what you can buy for next to nothing in an Asian food store: cassia bark, star anise, kecap manis, ponzu sauce – the list is endless. And once you've tried these ingredients, using them in your cooking will become second nature, and you'll be surprised at how they can spice up an everyday meal.

Dos and don'ts for a well-stocked pantry

Make sure your pantry is stocked with well-chosen staples – that way you can always rustle up something good to eat (and it's amazing how something like an excellent extra virgin olive oil can elevate a simple meal to restaurant quality standards).

No self-respecting pantry should be without the following:

- sea salt (not iodised table salt), fresh peppercorns and a pepper mill

- top quality extra virgin olive oil (the best you can afford – make sure you taste-test oils before buying to discover their diverse range of flavours), aged balsamic vinegar, white- or red-wine vinegar

- 'neutral' cooking oil – my shorthand for oils such as vegetable oil, canola oil, safflower oil and mild peanut oil, that are good for grilling or frying as they don't have a strong flavour to impart to food

- good quality canned tomatoes (preferably an Italian brand)

- dried pasta, rice (long-grain and risotto rice such as arborio, vialone or carnaroli)

- a hunk of real Italian parmesan cheese

- soy sauce, oyster sauce, fish sauce, sesame oil, Shaohsing rice wine

- anchovies (preferably salted, not in oil), black olives, capers.

Now, being a food snob is one thing, but some foods are nothing short of a sin against nature. If the following items never, ever make it into your kitchen, your life, or at least your stomach, you'll be all the better for it:

- ready-grated parmesan cheese – stale, sour, horrible stuff that comes in those 'convenient' cardboard shakers from the supermarket. This has nothing to do with actual cheese: buy a piece of real parmesan and a grater instead.

- stock cubes – are there any natural ingredients in these things? There's no excuse for them, as you can now buy premium quality ready-made stocks from butchers and specialty stores, and at a pinch you'll get away with the ones in Tetra Paks from the supermarket.

- ready-made salad dressings – why do these exist? Some good extra virgin olive oil, aged balsamic vinegar, salt and pepper are all you need to make the perfect vinaigrette (see page 208).

- Basa fillets – these should be known as Mekong River catfish, but who would buy them then? The worst of the low-grade imports, these are most likely what is in your kids' fish and chips. They're the greatest rort since people found out what was in chicken nuggets, and the manufacturers had to put actual meat in them instead.

- truffle oil – granted, this is a leap to the other end of the culinary scale, but truffle oil is simply the work of the devil: never, ever use it. If 99 per cent of chefs don't understand that it can only enhance a dish if used by the drop instead of the spoonful, how could you hope to?

What is this thing called, love?

One of the difficulties in navigating your way round the world of food is the variations in terminology when it comes to produce. It's bad enough when we can't agree with the Poms (they call snow peas mange tout) or the Septics (who call coriander cilantro), but even here at home confusion reigns when it comes to some types of food.

Take meat for example. What I call lamb loin, my local butcher calls lamb backstrap; sirloin can be New York cut, strip loin, porterhouse or even entrecote; and lamb fillets might also be called tenderloins. Good communication is the key here – describe to your butcher exactly what you have in mind (draw a diagram if it helps!), and they will advise you.

Shallots are the worst. The small French variety that look like they're wrapped in brown paper are called golden shallots, and their cousins, the red Thai variety, are known as red shallots. These are not to be confused with spring onions, the long, skinny green things with white tips (sometimes known as scallions or green onions), or salad onions, that have a large, rounded white bulb at the end. It's a bit like deciphering the scrum laws in rugby – I've followed and played the game for forty years and I still don't have a clue.

If you've cooked one risotto, you've cooked 'em all

One of the great things about learning to cook is that once you've mastered a technique, you can adapt it to make a whole variety of dishes, therefore impressing the pants off anyone who thought you were just a beginner.

Risotto is a great example. Once you've cooked, say, an asparagus risotto a few times, you'll understand how to achieve that slightly soupy consistency and you'll get the rice cooked perfectly every time, with just the right amount of bite. Then, to the standard 'base' of onion or leek, risotto rice and stock (usually chicken), instead of asparagus you could add fennel, roasted pumpkin, zucchini, peas or any veg that takes your fancy. You could also try using a fish stock instead of chicken and add any fresh fish or shellfish to make a seafood risotto.

Frittata is another one – the idea is basically lots of eggs with a bit of cheese and your choice of extra ingredients added, then it's fried very slowly in a pan until the egg has set. The list of options is endless: carrot, onion and zucchini; caramelised onion and rosemary; leftover spag bol; red capsicum, corn and basil; goat's curd and sage; tomato and pancetta . . . just walk around a good food market for inspiration.

Butter sauces are a bit passé now, mainly because they contain too much, well, butter, but it's not like you're going to eat them three times a day, are you? They add a nice bit of richness to grilled meat and fish if that's the effect you're after. You can add anything to the basic butter sauce – fresh herbs work well, especially sorrel, dill, basil, oregano, marjoram or thyme. You could even cross cultures and use ingredients like ginger and lemongrass, which would go well with fish.

The recipes in this book will help you get the basics right, then you can start exploring with all sorts of flavours and ingredients that you enjoy.

No one needs an Acme automatic watermelon-seed remover

Given the divorce rate and the number of guys who are living on their own these days, a lot of people have to set up a kitchen from scratch. I know that I did, second-time around. So, what are the essential tools of the trade in the kitchen?

Growing up, my family's kitchen was full of every useless plastic gadget ever made (certainly all those made by K-Tel and advertised on TV – Mum loved a gadget). But really, setting up a kitchen should be the opposite of this – it should be all about just two words: simplicity and quality.

But before you head to the shops, have a good look around your kitchen – the amount of bench or storage space you have will be the deciding factor on how much stuff you should buy. How big the oven is will tell you how big your baking dishes should be (and save you an embarrassing trip back to exchange them). And you need to consider the sort of things you'll actually cook: I rarely bake cakes and don't make my own bread, so I don't need a whole range of different-sized cake tins and I've never owned a Mixmaster.

You can pay a fortune for top-of-the-range stainless-steel saucepans with copper bases and cast-iron handles. If you can afford them and you're passionate about cooking, go for it. But, at more approachable prices, look for basic, good quality stainless-steel pots and pans, and get them in at least three sizes. (There's a good reason why professional kitchens are full of stainless-steel equipment – it is durable and doesn't absorb anything. It's also surprisingly inexpensive.)

Advances in technology have improved non-stick cookware enormously (though I wouldn't always believe those ten-year guarantees on some non-stick frying pans). Despite my cynicism, you can't do without one small and one large non-stick frying pan, and non-stick baking dishes with roasting racks are a godsend.

Buying a set of knives is a lot like buying clothes. The sky is pretty much the limit, price-wise, but you need some that you're personally comfortable with. Again, quality is the key; you're better off buying two or three very good knives than ten ordinary ones. Look for stainless-steel knives with a high carbon content – this makes them easier to sharpen and they'll hold their edge longer. Large stainless-steel serving spoons, ladles, whisks, strainers and sieves are also important to have, as is a decent-sized stockpot that doubles as a pan to cook your pasta in (but make sure it fits under your rangehood – another potential trap for young players). And, of course, a couple of chopping boards, a salad spinner, some solid kitchen scales and a stack of stainless-steel bowls in different sizes are all essential.

Personally, I swear by a rice cooker – they're only about fifty bucks, and rice is tricky to get right without one. A good food processor is also important, but don't just buy the first one you see. Check how easy they are to operate and how solid the top feels. A stab blender (a one-handed version of a food processor) is great for whipping up quick meals and is much easier to clean than a food processor – just make sure that you buy a deep cylindrical stainless-steel bowl to use with it.

You can't eat the tablecloth...

This is one of my favourite expressions of my old man's, and I agree with his sentiment entirely. Some people put more effort into the table setting and decoration than they do the food; personally, I don't give a stuff about that sort of thing. Make the food the hero – and for the rest, here are my tips on keeping it simple.

I think plates and bowls should be big and white and solid. I like cutlery that is plain and heavy, yet comfortable in the hand. Water glasses should be nice and big to save re-filling all the time, and wine glasses should be plain with fine rims. Look for wine glasses that are big enough to allow the wine room to breathe and be sloshed around, and that are crystal-clear so that you can see the wine. (Is there anything dumber than coloured wine glasses, or worse, metal ones that prevent you seeing the wine and actually interfere with the flavour?) And they might be a pain in the neck, but cloth serviettes are so much nicer than paper ones.

Outside of these fundamental things, I suggest that you let someone else worry about candles, flowers, place cards and anything else not to do with food.

Timing is everything

Cooking for friends is fun, but it's more fun if you've given it a bit of thought to make sure things go smoothly. Thinking the meal through beforehand will make the whole experience a lot more enjoyable for you and your guests.

First off, you'll need a shopping list – it's really boring having to run back to the shops to get the one thing that you forgot. Instead of the usual stream-of-consciousness list that most of us make, with no order or logical sequence to the items, try this: make six columns on a page – one for fruit and veg, one for meat, one for seafood, one for deli items, one for supermarket stuff and one for your cupboards at home (to check that you really have what you think you have). Then go through each recipe and write the ingredients in the appropriate columns, tick off the items you already have in the cupboard, and go forth and shop! This list takes no more time to make than an ordinary list, and makes shopping a hell of a lot more efficient.

Then you'll want to figure out which plates and serving dishes you need to have out, so you're not climbing in the back of cupboards and brushing the cobwebs off your fancy platters at the last minute. Make sure the table is set properly – the food that you've slaved over will get cold pretty quickly while your guests watch you scrambling for salt and pepper, serviettes, water, wine glasses and bread rolls. If the first course is served hot, get everybody sitting down, with a drink in front of them, before you even think about bringing the food to the table.

You'll also need to have a think about how much time each element of the meal will take to cook. For instance, when you're having a roast, you wouldn't put the broccoli on until the meat was out of the oven, well-rested and about to be carved, would you? Writing a menu for your guests would be incredibly wanky, but I always write one for myself, listing the components of each dish and the order in which I need to cook them. This really comes in handy if you like to have a few drinks while you cook (every chef's prerogative) – things can get a bit hazy after the fifth glass of wine. It may also prevent those inevitable slip-ups, such as discovering the watercress that was supposed to go with the prawns, still in the fridge the next morning.

The rules of matching food and wine

The first rule is: there are no rules. People get so hung up about what should go with what, when it should really be about your own personal taste. A few years ago, I read a book called *Red Wine with Fish: The New Art of Matching Wine with Food*, which challenged all the so-called 'rules' and explored some very left-field alternatives (some of which worked and some didn't, but the point was that the authors, like me, were pissed off by the assumption that there were 'rules' in the first place).

The important thing is to make a conscious decision about what you're going to serve with what, rather than grabbing the first bottle you see at the wine shop. Start by asking yourself a few pertinent questions.

Do you prefer red or white with veal? Which reds do you like best with slow-cooked meats? What's good with spicy Asian food?

As a bloke who has eaten an awful lot of food and drunk a river of wine over the years, I've got a smidge of experience in putting the two together, and so here are my thoughts on what tastes good with what. But don't just take my word for it – go ahead and experiment to figure it out for yourself.

I like a fresh young riesling or semillon with cold shellfish. A chardonnay or an older riesling or semillon (which I love but no one else seems to), work with warm shellfish and fish dishes, as well as vegetable and seafood risottos.  A viognier can go well with lighter seafood and vegetable dishes. I'm a fan of riesling with roast chook, and maybe a chardy with busier chicken dishes, but I'm the wrong man to talk to about sav blanc – I just don't like the stuff. For me, most whites don't really work with tuna; I prefer a pinot or a young, peppery shiraz. And one rule I do follow is matching pinot noir with duck, especially Chinese duck. If you need proof, make the pilgrimage to Melbourne's Flower Drum restaurant and wallow in the experience.

Spicy food is hard. I can never figure out how anybody could order a big woody chardonnay to go with chilli crab. I find that a young crisp white or a young shiraz will do the trick. And there is always beer.

Match cabernet-shiraz blends or one of the great range of new Italian varietals with different red meats – experimenting is half the fun. I find older reds sit nicely with slow braises, and younger ones go best with grills. (Though I could happily drink Hill of Grace, Bass Phillip Premium Pinot or Grange with a bag of Smith's chips.)

Matching the sweetness of a dessert with the sweetness of the wine is difficult – one always tends to be sweeter than the other. Experiment as much as you can. I like a little cognac, liqueur muscat, tokay or sweet port with chocolate puddings and cakes, and a lot of the same stuff afterwards. And I suggest that you try rich whites like chardonnay to go with soft cheeses, though it can be a nuisance going back to white at the end of a meal when you're in red mode.

We're constantly being exposed to new ideas and your palate will evolve and change, so the best thing you can do is work out what *you* like, and remember – there are no wrong answers.

Leaving home

Leaving home

Let's start at the very beginning, as Julie Andrews sang a long time ago. This chapter provides some basic ideas for those young blokes, or even older blokes, who, up until now, have regarded food preparation as buying a frozen meal and sticking it in the microwave or dialling Domino's. Cooking well is all about building confidence, and the key is to start with easy dishes – no one expects you to be making soufflés on day one.

The first step to culinary greatness is making sure you always use top-notch produce. Find an excellent fishmonger, a quality butcher and deli, and the best greengrocer in your area. To get you started, there is nothing wrong with simply buying fabulous fresh produce and doing bugger-all to it – better that than being overly ambitious and things not coming off. Try dishes so simple they don't even need a recipe: buffalo mozzarella served with sliced ripe tomatoes, some fresh basil and a drizzle of really good extra virgin olive oil (the classic Caprese salad); a hunk of top quality parmesan cheese served with fresh crusty bread and figs or slices of ripe pear; or fresh fruit and berries for dessert with real cream or some thick, luscious organic yoghurt. Then move on to a basic stir-fry, pasta dish or roast, and once you've mastered these you can gradually build up your repertoire. You'll soon find that mussels with white wine and garlic aren't that different to mussels with tomato and chilli sauce, and roast chook isn't a huge leap from roast lamb. Once you get going, you'll gain the confidence to experiment with a variety of ingredients, and you'll soon be ready for bigger and better things – like food to seduce, but more on that later.

Before you start, you'll need some decent kitchen equipment, though you don't need to go over the top. Beginners especially should have a good read through the hints on page 8 on setting up your kitchen.

'No one expects you to be making soufflés on day one.'

Pasta with leek, tomato and pancetta sauce (see page 26)

MUSSELS IN WHITE WINE AND GARLIC

Serves 4

Mussels are a joy to cook. They transform before your eyes in just minutes, and they're delicious. I have cooked them probably a dozen different ways over the years, and this is the simplest way and just about the best.

Try to buy live mussels if you can, or the Kinkawooka Boston Bay mussels from South Australia, which you'll find vacuum-packed in the supermarket or at your fishmongers.

2 tablespoons olive oil
3 cloves garlic, finely sliced
2 kg small black mussels, 'beards' removed,
    any open shells discarded
½ cup dry white wine
½ cup chopped flat-leaf parsley
freshly ground black pepper
crusty bread, to serve

Heat the oil in a large stockpot over low heat and fry the garlic. As soon as the garlic starts to sizzle, throw in all the mussels and pour in the wine. Cover and leave to simmer for 2 minutes. Add the parsley and black pepper, and give everything a gentle stir. Cover again and simmer until all the shells have opened, then take off the heat straightaway and serve.

MANGO CHILLI DIPPING SAUCE, TO SERVE WITH PRAWNS

Makes about 1 cup of sauce

This is a five-minute recipe that oozes with the flavours of an Australian summer. It's a great show-off dish – the sauce tastes so good that people will assume it's much more work than it really is.

1 ripe mango, peeled and stone removed
½ large red chilli, very finely chopped
large pinch freshly ground black pepper
2 teaspoons lime juice
½ cup finely sliced mint leaves

Purée the mango flesh to a fine pulp using a food processor or a stab blender, transfer to a bowl and stir all the other ingredients through.

Serve alongside fresh, cooked prawns.

 HOT TIP If you're feeling lazy, don't bother chopping the chilli and mint by hand, just throw the lot into the food processor. The texture will be slightly different, but equally delicious.

RAS EL HANOUT PRAWNS

Serves 4 as an entrée

Meaning 'top of the shop' in Arabic, ras el hanout is a blend of Middle-eastern spices, traditionally a mixture of the best ones the seller has on offer. Blends can contain anything from a dozen spices to over one hundred.

This is a really impressive entrée or could even work as finger food.

16–20 green (raw) king prawns
50 g butter, melted
2–3 tablespoons ras el hanout
sea salt and lemon wedges, to serve

To prepare the prawns, twist off the head and peel off the shell, leaving the last section of the tail on. With a sharp knife, cut almost all the way through the back of the prawns so they 'butterfly' out and lie flat, and remove the dark intestinal tract.

Place the prawns on a baking tray covered with foil, brush them with melted butter and sprinkle the ras el hanout over the top. Cook the prawns under a very hot grill without turning them, until they are opaque, and serve topped with a sprinkle of sea salt and a lemon wedge on the side.

BREAD AND TOMATO SALAD

Serves 4 as an entrée

I once made this simple salad for my old mate Dirty Lizzy, who is such an ordinary cook that she forgot to turn the oven on at one of her dinner parties . . . not a good look. She liked this salad so much she asked for the recipe (all of five ingredients – I refuse to count the salt and pepper), and then proceeded to ring me back four times to check and double-check them. I promise you won't find it that hard.

This salad is perfect as an entrée or an accompaniment to pasta or grilled meats. You absolutely need fabulous, ripe tomatoes for this to work.

4 ripe tomatoes, cut into chunks
1 day-old Italian rosetta roll, or similar, cut into chunks
about 20 basil leaves, torn
⅓ cup extra virgin olive oil
2 tablespoons balsamic vinegar
plenty of sea salt and freshly ground black pepper

Mix all the ingredients together in a large bowl. Add more oil and vinegar if required and serve immediately.

 When it comes to the bread in this salad, fresh is definitely not best – it would be way too mushy. The trick is remembering to buy your bread the day before.

VEAL LIMONE
(VEAL WITH LEMON SAUCE)
Serves 2

Good food doesn't get much easier than this.
You just need to buy top quality veal and have
the confidence not to overcook it. And with any
sauce finished with butter, the important thing
is to remove it from the heat once you have
added the butter, or the texture will be cactus.

about 60 g butter
4 milk-fed veal steaks, about ⅔ cm thick
sea salt and freshly ground black pepper, to taste
2 tablespoons lemon juice
1 teaspoon very finely chopped flat-leaf parsley

Melt ½ teaspoon of the butter in a large non-stick frying
pan over high heat. Season the veal steaks on both sides
with salt and pepper. Place the steaks in the hot pan and
cook quickly – a minute on each side should be plenty.

Remove the steaks from the pan and place on warm
plates. Add the lemon juice, the parsley and the rest of
the butter to the pan, removing it from the heat as you
do, and swirl the butter around the pan to melt it.

Spoon the sauce over the steaks and serve.

 It's worth finding a butcher who sells real
veal – young, pale and pink, not dark red.

BAKED CHICKEN WITH
WHITE WINE AND ROSEMARY
Serves 4

This is the training-wheels dish from my
cooking classes – it is almost impossible to
screw up. You won't ever end up with dry,
tasteless chicken, because the liquid in the
dish is absorbed by the meat. Magic.

You'll need 5 minutes to throw it all together,
then it marinates for half an hour (time for a
drink), and cooks for 45 minutes or so (time to
polish off the bottle).

1 free-range or organic chicken, cut into 8 pieces (ask
   your butcher to do this for you), or 8 chicken thighs
2 large desiree or other waxy potatoes, peeled
   and cut into small chunks
½ large bulb fennel, trimmed and roughly
   chopped (optional)
crusty bread, to serve

MARINADE
4 sprigs rosemary, leaves picked
2 tablespoons roughly chopped flat-leaf parsley
½ cup extra virgin olive oil
½–¾ cup dry white wine
½ cup freshly grated parmesan cheese
2 teaspoons sea salt
½ teaspoon freshly ground black pepper

Place the chicken pieces (skin-side up), the potatoes
and the fennel, if using, in a large baking dish and add the
marinade ingredients, stirring well. Set aside to marinate
for about half an hour. Preheat the oven to 200°C.

Place the dish in the hot oven and cook for
45 minutes–1 hour. Most of the oil and wine will have
been absorbed by the chicken and vegetables, and the
top should be nicely browned.

Serve with plenty of crusty bread.

PASTA WITH VEAL RAGU
Serves an army

Spag bol is supposed to be the nation's most-cooked dish, and while the mince, onion and tomato combo is almost foolproof, it's usually pretty ordinary. Try this very simple slow braise as a stylish alternative.

Once you understand the basics of a braise or casserole like this, you can make a million variations. It's always about lightly dusting the meat in seasoned flour and browning it in oil, then combining it with vegetables and some liquid and cooking it slowly. And it's always better cooked a day ahead and gently reheated.

1 kg veal, cut into 2 cm cubes
⅓ cup plain flour, seasoned with sea salt
    and freshly ground black pepper
⅓ cup olive oil
1 stalk celery, finely sliced
1 large brown onion, diced
2 cloves garlic, finely sliced
1 × 500 ml bottle passata (puréed tomatoes)
1 piece orange peel, about 2 cm × 4 cm,
    white pith removed
2 tablespoons chopped flat-leaf parsley,
    plus extra to garnish
1 fresh bay leaf
1 tablespoon tomato paste (optional)
1 cup dry white wine

TO SERVE
100 g per person good quality dried pasta
½ cup freshly grated parmesan cheese

Put the meat in a large plastic bag (check there are no holes) along with the seasoned flour and shake to thoroughly coat the meat. Heat half the oil in a non-stick frying pan over high heat and brown the meat in batches.

In a large casserole dish, heat the remaining oil over medium heat and fry the celery, onion and garlic until softened, then add the browned meat, passata, orange peel, parsley, bay leaf, tomato paste (if using), and the white wine. Add enough water to just cover the ingredients, and season with salt and pepper. Bring to the boil, then reduce to a low heat and simmer for 2 hours.

When ready to serve, bring a large saucepan of salted water to the boil, slide in the pasta and cook until al dente, then drain, reserving a little of the cooking water. Stir the cooked pasta through the sauce, adding a little of the cooking water if necessary.

Serve with freshly grated parmesan sprinkled on top.

ITALIAN PAN-FRIED CHICKEN

Serves 4

This dish will transport those of you old enough to remember back to the simple Italian restaurants of days gone by. The principle is very straightforward, really: you brown the chicken pieces well to add flavour and colour, then half fry/half steam them, resulting in wonderfully tender meat that would break the Colonel's heart.

This goes beautifully with crispy roast potatoes and a green salad.

1 small free-range or organic chicken, cut into 8 pieces (ask your butcher to do this for you), then the breasts cut in half
¼ cup plain flour, seasoned with salt and pepper
⅓ cup olive oil
2 tablespoons finely chopped rosemary
½ cup dry white wine

Put the chicken pieces in a large plastic bag (check there are no holes) along with the seasoned flour and shake to thoroughly coat the meat. Heat the oil in a large frying pan over high heat, and brown the chicken pieces in batches, turning to make sure all the sides are browned. Sprinkle over the rosemary and add the white wine, reducing the heat to medium.

Cut out two rounds of greaseproof paper to fit snugly in the pan and press the paper directly on top of the contents of the pan. Simmer for about 15 minutes, then remove the paper and insert the point of a sharp knife into the thickest part of the chicken. If the juices run clear, it is cooked. If they are pink or bloody, replace paper and cook for another 5 minutes or so.

Serve the chicken with the juices spooned over.

 Browning means what it says. Cook the chicken over high heat to colour and caramelise the skin, and add miles of flavour.

PORK AND SNAKE BEAN STIR-FRY

Serves 4

Here's a dish that's fantastically quick and easy. Snake beans can be a bit hard to find, but they have a really crunchy texture that works well with the minced pork and the saltiness of the sauces. You could substitute normal green beans at a pinch.

Rice cookers are the one gadget I swear by, so do yourself a favour and invest in one (I've included a method to cook rice here for the gadgetly-challenged, though).

2 cups long-grain rice
2 tablespoons peanut oil
4 spring onions, white and pale green parts only, sliced
1 medium-sized red chilli, seeds removed, finely sliced
2 cloves garlic, crushed
500 g premium pork mince
about 12 snake beans, cut into 4 cm lengths
1 tablespoon soy sauce
¼ cup oyster sauce
2 teaspoons fish sauce

Bring 4 cups of water to the boil in a saucepan with a tight-fitting lid. Add the rice, turn the heat down to its lowest setting, cover and cook for 17–20 minutes, or until the rice is cooked.

Meanwhile, get your wok nice and hot, then heat the oil and add the spring onions, chilli, garlic and pork mince. Stir-fry until the mince has changed colour, then add the beans and the sauces and simmer for 2 minutes. Serve hot with the rice.

ROAST LAMB
Serves 4 easily

A lot of blokes really miss the family roast when they leave home, and it's right behind cooking a good steak on their To Do list in the kitchen.

I still remember a desperate Christmas a quarter of a century ago with my future-wife's family at a well-meaning aunt's place in Melbourne. It was stinking hot and I had to wear long pants (not happy). The tucker that day has become the stuff of family legend; I reckon the roast went on at six that morning and the broccoli had started boiling at lunch-time on Christmas Eve – tough, grey meat, and vegetables that made the meat look good.

Timing is everything with a roast and practice is the only way to get it right. Make sure you are ridiculously generous with every-thing, including the gravy, because there's never too much traditional roast dinner. And remember, the broccoli goes into the boiling water as you start carving the meat . . .

1 medium-sized leg of lamb (about 2 kg)
⅓ cup extra virgin olive oil
sea salt and freshly ground black pepper
2 cloves garlic, cut lengthways into 4–6 slices
1 stalk rosemary
4 desiree or other waxy potatoes, peeled and cut
   into half or thirds
about 500 g pumpkin, cut into chunks
2 medium-sized parsnips, peeled and halved lengthways
2 medium-sized carrots, peeled and halved lengthways
2 tablespoons plain flour
2 cups shelled green peas
about 24 green beans
½ cup good quality ready-made veal stock diluted with
   ½ cup water *or* 1 cup Homemade Chicken Stock
   (see page 208)
1 small head broccoli, broken into small florets

Preheat the oven to 190°C. Rub the lamb all over with half the oil and season with salt and pepper. With the point of a sharp knife, make about ten evenly-spaced incisions in the top of the lamb, about a centimetre deep. Push a slice of garlic and a sprig of rosemary into each incision, and place the lamb in a small baking dish. Place the spuds, pumpkin, parsnips and carrots in another small baking dish, and toss through the remaining olive oil and a tablespoon of sea salt.

Roast the lamb and vegetables in the oven for 1 hour. Check to see if the vegetables are cooked – if so, remove them, cover with foil and set aside to keep warm. If not, give them a few more minutes. Cook the meat for another 15 minutes, then check for done-ness by inserting a skewer into the thickest part of the leg; if the juices are blood-red and the meat is still very soft, it needs more time – try another 10 minutes before checking again. If the juices are pink and the meat is fairly firm, you should have a perfectly cooked roast. Meanwhile, half-fill a saucepan with salted water and bring to the boil, ready for your green veg.

Once the roast is cooked to your liking, transfer the meat to a chopping board, loosely cover with foil and let it stand for 10 minutes.

Place the meat-baking dish on the stove over medium heat and add the flour, stirring vigorously with a wooden spoon to loosen all the yummy brown sticky bits on the bottom of the pan. Now is when your peas and beans should go on – add them to the pan of boiling water.

Cook the flour for a minute or so, until lightly browned, then add the stock, reduce the heat to a simmer and keep stirring until you have a smooth gravy, adding water or more flour as needed to get the right consistency. Pour into a gravy boat and scrape in every last drop.

Now is when your broccoli should go on – add it to the pan of boiling water with the peas and beans, and cook until just tender.

Carve the lamb into large slices, giving everyone bits from different parts of the leg, and serve generous portions of everything else, with the gravy on the side – and plenty of great Australian shiraz.

PASTA WITH LEEK, TOMATO AND PANCETTA SAUCE

Serves 4

I went to heaps of cooking classes in my twenties and so was lucky enough to learn the basics from many of Australia's top chefs. This pasta sauce, a version of one I saw Steve Manfredi make at a class, is the easiest you can do – the sauce cooks faster than the spaghetti. The quality of the ingredients will make or break this dish, so make sure you buy the best you can afford.

Drizzling good quality extra virgin olive oil over the pasta just before serving takes the dish to a whole new dimension.

2 thin slices pancetta, chopped
2 tablespoons extra virgin olive oil, plus more
    for drizzling
2 leeks, white part only, sliced
3 cloves garlic, finely sliced
8 ripe roma tomatoes, cut into quarters, seeds
    removed, then quarters cut in half lengthways
sea salt and freshly ground black pepper
1 cup torn basil leaves
400 g good quality dried pasta
½ cup freshly grated parmesan cheese

Fry the pancetta in the olive oil in a heavy-based frying pan until golden brown, then add the leeks and garlic and cook until they soften and just start to colour. Add the tomatoes and some salt and pepper, and cook until the tomatoes start to break up. Remove from the heat and stir through the basil.

Meanwhile, bring a large saucepan of salted water to the boil, slide in the pasta and cook until al dente. Stir the just-cooked pasta through the sauce, add a good glug of olive oil, spoon into bowls and top with a sprinkling of parmesan cheese.

HONEYDEW MELON AND ROSEWATER SOUP

Serves 4

I first had this dessert at a Turkish restaurant in Buenos Aires a decade ago, and the proprietor thought it was the cleverest thing he'd ever seen (and he charged accordingly). The combination of the Turkish Delight flavour of the rosewater with the clean taste of honeydew was brilliant, and it's such a simple dish that anyone can try it.

You could trick it up with some raspberry purée and fresh berries, but it is perfectly delicious as is – just make sure you serve it well chilled.

You can buy rosewater at any good delicatessen.

½ large honeydew melon, peeled and
    seeds removed, cut into chunks
2 tablespoons sugar dissolved in ½ cup
    water (sugar syrup)
1 teaspoon rosewater, and a little more
    to taste if necessary

In a food processor, purée the melon, sugar syrup and rosewater to a smooth, runny liquid. Taste, and add more rosewater as necessary. Set aside in the fridge to chill.

 While this is a delicious dessert soup, you don't want a bucket of it. Small serving bowls are the go – I've even served it in shot glasses at a drinks party.

PEACH AND
RASPBERRY CRUMBLE

Serves 6

Crumbles are basically fruit and/or berries sprinkled with a crumble mixture and bunged in a hot oven. Once you've mastered the basic principles, the options are endless. Apples or pears with sultanas and cinnamon, peaches or mangoes with strawberries, raspberries or blueberries; they all work. This is a dessert for blokes who reckon they can't cook.

butter, for greasing
6 peaches, peeled and sliced into thick chunks
1 punnet raspberries
½ cup plain flour
¾ cup brown sugar
1 teaspoon cinnamon
50 g butter, chopped into small pieces
ice cream or cream, to serve

Preheat the oven to 225°C. Grease a small shallow baking dish (approx 30 cm × 20 cm) with butter and spread the peaches and raspberries over the base.

Mix the flour, brown sugar and cinnamon in a bowl and add the butter, rubbing the mixture with your fingers until the butter is roughly incorporated – the texture should be quite lumpy.

Spread this crumble mixture evenly over the fruit and bake for 20 minutes or until the top is brown and crunchy.

Serve warm with ice cream or pure, thick cream.

FRENCH TOAST WITH QUICK POACHED STRAWBERRIES

Serves 2 for a decadent breakfast or dessert

This one's a bit messy, but it's a 10 minute job, start to finish – and we love that. You should be able to find a loaf of brioche at your local bakers or patisserie.

2 organic or free-range eggs

2 tablespoons thick cream

1 teaspoon vanilla extract

60 g butter, plus more for cooking

1 punnet ripe strawberries, washed, tops removed

1 teaspoon very finely grated orange zest

2 tablespoons caster sugar

¼ cup fresh orange juice

1 teaspoon Grand Marnier, brandy or rum (optional)

4 thick slices brioche

cream or custard, to serve

Beat the eggs, cream and vanilla together in a bowl.

Melt a teaspoon of the butter in a small pan and add the strawberries and orange zest, cooking for about 30 seconds over low heat. Add the sugar and allow to dissolve, before pouring in the orange juice and liqueur or spirit, if using, and cooking for another minute.

Melt the rest of the butter in a non-stick frying pan. One by one, briefly immerse the brioche slices in the egg and cream mixture, then gently fry them. Place 2 slices of French toast on each plate and spoon the poached strawberries and sauce over. Top with a little cream or custard if you like.

 Once you've dipped the brioche slices in the egg and cream mixture, quickly get them into the pan otherwise they'll turn to mush before your eyes.

The humble bumnut. We assume they're a piece of cake to cook, but whichever way you like your eggs, they can be tricky unless you know a few trade secrets.

First, you need to start with a really good egg. Organic eggs from a small, local producer are best, followed by organic eggs from a commercial producer and free-range eggs, then eggs from a poor old battery chook.

Always make sure your eggs are fresh. No matter where it comes from, a stale googie is still a stale googie.

Although we all like our eggs cooked differently, for the purposes of this demonstration let's assume that just-set whites and runny, golden yolks are the goal for boiled, fried and poached eggs, and that light and fluffy is what we want from our scrambled eggs and omelettes.

BOILED EGGS

Place an egg in a saucepan and cover with cold water. Bring the water to a boil and cook for 3 minutes, then remove the egg from the pan, whip off the top, sprinkle with just a little sea salt and freshly ground black pepper, and serve in your favourite egg cup with some buttered toast soldiers. The breakfast of champions!

FRIED EGGS

Besides top quality, fresh eggs, you need a truly-ruly non-stick frying pan to make the best fried eggs. (Non-stick pans lose their non-stickiness fairly quickly as a rule – whether you get a cheapie from the supermarket or fork out for a super-duper flash one, neither will last forever unfortunately.) Melt a little butter, neutral oil (see page 6) or olive oil in the frying pan and gently break an egg into the pan. When the egg white is just firm, carefully flip the egg with a spatula, and cook for a further 20 seconds before transferring to a plate to serve.

POACHED EGGS

Poaching eggs is actually really simple, if you follow two golden rules. Don't have the water boiling too hard (a rolling boil is too strong) and don't use a shallow frying pan – you need a nice deep pan to poach properly. Then, it's as simple as adding a teaspoon of vinegar to some salted, barely simmering water and gently breaking an egg into a cup before sliding it into the pan. When the egg is just cooked (about 3–4 minutes), carefully remove it with a slotted spoon, and serve.

A good egg

SCRAMBLED EGGS

Scrambled eggs were elevated to an art form when Bill Granger opened his first cafe in Sydney's Darlinghurst all those years ago. His creamy scrambled eggs have become his signature, along with great cafe food, pastel T-shirts and that cheesy grin.

You can cook scrambled eggs two ways – really fast or really slow – but there's no middle ground. The fine chef Damien Pignolet taught me to cook them slowly over low, low heat (virtually just a lit match), which does create an amazing texture, but you'll grow old and die waiting for them to cook, so let's go with the quicker way.

To serve one person, break two or three eggs into a bowl, add a tablespoon of cream, season with sea salt and beat well. Now's the time to throw the bread in the toaster.

Heat your truly-ruly non-stick frying pan, add a teaspoon of butter and, as it starts to melt, add a tablespoon of cream. Pour in the egg mixture and cook, stirring occasionally, until the eggs are just beginning to set. The secret to perfectly cooked scrambled eggs is to remove them from the heat at this point, as they will keep cooking even when they're on your plate (and no, you can't leave them cooking to go and butter your toast or you'll miss the moment). Top with freshly ground black pepper and serve.

OMELETTES

Like scrambled eggs, less is more when cooking an omelette. Many chefs will use the 'omelette test' to tell if aspiring cooks really know what they're doing – even the best will stuff it up sometimes.

Have your filling ready to go (you could use fresh herbs, grated cheese, diced ham and tomato, sautéed mushrooms: the list is endless – just don't be too generous with the filling). Beat two or three eggs together and add a bit of salt. Melt a teaspoon of butter in a non-stick frying pan, tilting the pan from side to side so that the butter coats the entire surface. Pour in the egg mixture and tilt the pan again so the egg covers the base of the pan. Cook for about 30 seconds, then gently push in the sides with a wooden spatula and tilt the pan so that the raw egg runs over the edges of the cooked egg. Cook for another minute or so, tilting the pan again. Add the filling to one half of the omelette, and gently fold over the other half, then slide it out on to a plate and serve.

Food to watch the footy with

Food to watch the footy with

Most blokes get on the phone for takeaway crap when their mates come round to watch a Significant Sporting Event on the telly (of which there are half a dozen most weekends). But why would you eat that stuff? The only reason I'm the size of one house and not the whole block is that I'm never guilty of darkening the towels at the Golden Arches, the Colonel's (remember when it was Kentucky *Fried* Chicken?) or any of the commercial pizza joints. The occasional greasy hamburger from your local milk bar is fine, because at least it has some flavour, but it's hardly the sort of thing to excite your mates, who, in most cases, will be male, hungry and very thirsty (and in my case, played the great game of rugby, and have between two and five Xs before the L on their shirt collars).

It might be stating the obvious, but cooking for your footy-watching mates is very different to cooking for a dinner party. The most important thing is that you're in front of the TV, not the stove. You don't want to be the bunny in the kitchen when the try of the century is scored. You've got plenty of time before the game, so do all your prep work then, and at half-time you can simply serve the food and top up the drinks.

Speaking of drinks, experience tells me that there's a pretty good chance your guests (and the cook) will wind up over-refreshed, so you need food that will soak up the booze. Forget sushi, steamed veggies or tofu – watching footy is a tofu-free zone. Delicate flavours, delicate presentation and, presumably, delicate conversation, are all out the window. You need recipes with strong flavours that can be dished up in a minute and eaten on your lap. I like slow-cooked meaty dishes that you can eat stuffed into a tortilla or bread roll. And forget about dessert – this is no time for sweet things. Give them red-wine-friendly cheese, crusty bread and, you guessed it, red wine.

Of course, if you're at the stage in proceedings when you're pulling the cork from the liqueur muscat bottle with your teeth, forget cooking altogether and dial for that pizza after all.

'You don't want to be the bunny in the kitchen when the try of the century is scored.'

Prawn cutlets
with rémoulade (see page 38)

37

PRAWN CUTLETS WITH RÉMOULADE

Serves 4 as finger food

You are spoiling your mates with these. Of course you can buy nasty little frozen crumbed prawn cutlets, but life is too short to eat crap.

As with anything that needs to be crumbed, you'll be up to your armpits in egg, flour and breadcrumbs in no time, but you can make these a couple of hours before the game, clean yourself up, and then just heat the oil at half-time and throw them in – they cook in just a couple of minutes. The only certainty here is that you can't cook as many as your mates can eat.

12 green (raw) king prawns
1 cup plain flour seasoned with 1 teaspoon sea salt
2 organic or free-range eggs, beaten
2 cups breadcrumbs
1 cup neutral oil (see page 6)
sea salt

RÉMOULADE
½ cup Homemade Mayonnaise (see page 208)
   or good quality ready-made mayonnaise
2 tablespoons Dijon mustard
2 teaspoons finely chopped capers
1 tablespoon finely chopped gherkins
1 tablespoon finely chopped chervil or tarragon
1 tablespoon lemon juice

To make the rémoulade, combine all the ingredients in a bowl and set aside.

To prepare the prawns, twist off the head and peel off the shell, leaving the last section of the tail on. With a sharp knife, cut almost all the way through the back of the prawns so they 'butterfly' out and lie flat, and remove the dark intestinal tract.

Arrange three bowls in front of you. Put the seasoned flour in one, the eggs mixed with a tablespoon of cold water in the second, and the breadcrumbs in the third. Take each prawn and dip it in the flour then the egg before thoroughly coating it with the breadcrumbs.

Heat a large wok or frying pan over high heat and add the oil, then fry the prawns until golden brown. Drain on paper towel and sprinkle with sea salt, then serve with the rémoulade.

FILO CHEESE TRIANGLES

Makes about 3 dozen

These are yummy and have a salty kick that is terrific with beer. The beauty of them is that you can make a batch before your mates arrive and serve them still warm from the oven, or you can cook them the day before and reheat them. Stranger things have happened than demolishing them cold with a hangover, too, but that's another chapter.

200 g ricotta cheese
200 g feta cheese
100 g freshly grated pecorino cheese
2 organic or free-range eggs
1 teaspoon fresh thyme leaves, chopped
pinch nutmeg
freshly ground black pepper, to taste
1 packet chilled, not frozen, filo pastry
   (you'll need about 12 sheets of pastry)
about 100 g butter, melted

Preheat the oven to 190°C. Drain any liquid from the ricotta and feta, mix the three cheeses together in a bowl, then add the eggs, thyme, nutmeg and pepper, and combine.

Working with one sheet of pastry at a time, cut each sheet into thirds lengthways. Brush the tops and sides of each with melted butter. Place a small teaspoon of the cheese mixture in the bottom left-hand corner of each strip of pastry, then fold the pastry over and over again, making a right-angled triangle each time. Assemble the rest of the triangles in the same way until all the filling is used up. Place them on baking trays lined with baking paper and cook for about 15 minutes, or until the pastry turns golden brown. If you are making them the day before and reheating them, they will need slightly less time in the oven.

 While you are assembling the triangles, keep the remaining filo sheets covered with a damp tea towel so they don't dry out and become brittle.

CHICKEN PIE

Serves 4–6

Every time I make this little beauty at my cooking classes, it unanimously wins the vote for favourite dish, so it must have something going for it.

This is best tackled when you've just made chicken stock for something else and you're left with a very cooked chook and some spare stock. From there, this very homely, not-so-flash-looking dish is a piece of cake to make.

2 cups Homemade Chicken Stock (see page 208)
3 tablespoons butter
1 large carrot, sliced
1–2 leeks, white part only, sliced
1 stalk celery, sliced
1 heaped tablespoon plain flour
sea salt and white pepper
about 15 button mushrooms, halved
1 tablespoon finely chopped fresh thyme,
    rosemary or flat-leaf parsley
1 cooked chicken, skin and fat discarded, meat removed
    from bones and cut or torn into bite-sized pieces
1 sheet frozen puff pastry, thawed
1 organic or free-range egg, beaten with
    a few drops of milk

Simmer the stock over medium heat until it has reduced by about a third.

Preheat the oven to 200°C. In a large, deep pan, melt 2 tablespoons of the butter, then throw in the carrot, leek and celery and cook until just starting to soften. Add the flour, plenty of sea salt and some white pepper and stir until the flour and butter are completely combined and have formed a paste (called a roux). Gradually add the warm reduced chicken stock and stir over a low heat until the stock is incorporated into the roux.

Meanwhile, brown the mushrooms in a separate pan in the remaining tablespoon of butter, then add to the pan along with the herbs and the chicken pieces.

Transfer the pie filling to a ceramic baking dish and top with the pastry sheet, trimming it so it hangs over the sides of the dish by about 1 cm. Pierce the middle of the pastry sheet with a knife to allow the steam to escape, brush with the egg and milk mixture (this gives it a nice, shiny surface), then pop the pie in the oven and bake for 20 minutes or until the pastry is golden brown.

HEARTY LAMB AND VEGETABLE SOUP

Serves 4–6

When does a soup stop being a soup and start being a casserole? This is not a delicate entrée to have before a big main course; it's a meal in itself, chock-full of meat and veg.

If you don't want to waste this on your footy-watching chums, it is a wonderful winter dish for the family.

1 tablespoon olive oil
1 lamb shoulder, about 1.3 kg
2 red onions, finely diced
2 large carrots, finely diced
2 stalks celery, sliced
1 bay leaf
1 clove garlic, sliced
sea salt and freshly ground black pepper
1 small parsnip, finely diced
some freshly grated parmesan cheese, to serve
about 8 sprigs fresh thyme, leaves picked, to serve

Heat the oil in a large stockpot and brown the lamb shoulder on all sides. Add half the diced onion, carrot and celery, along with the bay leaf, garlic and 2 large pinches of sea salt. Add enough cold water to completely cover the ingredients, bring to a boil, then reduce the heat and simmer for 1½ hours, skimming off any fat or scum that forms on top.

Once cooked, transfer the lamb to a chopping board and, using two forks, shred all the meat from the bones, discarding all the fat and skin. Strain the stock into another saucepan, discarding the cooked vegetables, and add the shredded meat to the pan. Return it to the heat and add the remaining vegetables, simmering until they are just cooked. Ladle the soup into bowls and top with some grated parmesan, a sprinkle of thyme leaves and some freshly ground black pepper.

CHILLI
Serves 6

There are a million different chilli recipes; this version is based on my friend Jill Dupleix's recipe from her now-old but still terrific book, *New Food*. I prefer to use plain old red kidney beans rather than black beans, and I've added tomato paste for richness and upped the amount of herbs.

With this amount of beans and onions, chilli is serious fart food. But as we all know, if you're watching the footy with the boys, farting is hysterically funny.

2–3 tablespoons neutral oil (see page 6)
3 cloves garlic, very finely diced
2 medium–large onions, finely diced
1 large red capsicum, white insides and
    seeds removed, finely diced
500 g minced beef
2 teaspoons ground cumin
2 teaspoons dried oregano
1 teaspoon chilli powder, or more to taste
1 teaspoon paprika
2 tablespoons tomato paste
1 × 400 g can diced tomatoes
½ teaspoon Tabasco sauce, plus extra to serve (optional)
150 ml ready-made beef stock diluted with 150 ml water
1 tablespoon sea salt
freshly ground black pepper
200 g dried red kidney beans, soaked in cold water
    for 6 hours or overnight
2 tablespoons finely chopped flat-leaf parsley
dry crackers, to serve

Heat the oil in a large, heavy-based saucepan and gently soften the garlic, onion and capsicum over low heat. Add the mince and dried spices and increase the heat, stirring until the meat starts to brown. Add the tomato paste, canned tomatoes, Tabasco sauce, beef stock, salt and pepper and stir to combine.

Drain the beans and add them to the pan, adding water to cover the ingredients if necessary. Bring to a boil, then simmer for 1–1½ hours, or until the beans are cooked but not mushy. Taste for seasoning and adjust as needed, then add the parsley and stir through.

Ladle the chilli into bowls and serve with dry crackers crumbled on top, and extra Tabasco for the heat freaks.

FIFTEEN-MINUTE BAKED BEANS
Serves 4

There are usually two extremes when it comes to baked beans. You can simply open a can of the lolly-flavoured commercial variety, or you can do it the 'proper' way and soak some dried beans all day then cook them for hours.

This solution is somewhere between the two, and is disgustingly bloody delicious.

Under no circumstances should you get yourself confused and serve this on a hot date – it's one for the chaps only. It's particularly good for breakfast during one of those 5 a.m. sporting telecasts from the other side of the world.

1 tablespoon olive oil
1 large clove garlic, crushed
1 small–medium red onion, finely diced
1 cup diced leg ham
1 × 400 g can diced tomatoes
1 cup tomato sauce
1 teaspoon dried mustard powder
2 tablespoons Worcestershire sauce
⅓ cup cider vinegar
½ teaspoon celery salt
¼ teaspoon cayenne pepper (optional)
1 tablespoon finely chopped flat-leaf parsley
2 × 400 g cans cannellini beans, drained and
    gently rinsed
sourdough toast, to serve

Heat the oil in a large frying pan, then add the garlic, onion and ham and cook until the onion is softened but not browned. Add all the other ingredients except the beans and simmer for 5 minutes, then toss in the beans and cook, stirring gently, for 5 minutes more.

Serve heaped into a shallow bowl alongside some sourdough toast.

SPANISH-STYLE MUSSELS WITH CHORIZO

Serves 4

You can knock this dish out during half-time in the footy or a cricket tea break, as long as you've done a bit of chopping and slicing beforehand. These are blokes' flavours: big, rich and unsubtle – quite like a lot of blokes I know, really.

300 g dried or fresh chorizo sausage, sliced

3 tablespoons olive oil

2 large brown onions, sliced

4 cloves garlic, sliced

2 green capsicums, white insides and seeds
    removed, cut into small pieces

2 teaspoons smoked paprika

½ teaspoon cayenne pepper (optional)

2 kg small black mussels, 'beards' removed,
    any open shells discarded

2 cups passata (puréed tomatoes)

1 cup dry white wine

1 cup chopped flat-leaf parsley

freshly ground black pepper

crusty bread, to serve

In a large stockpot with a lid, fry the chorizo in the olive oil until lightly browned. Add the onion, garlic and capsicum and cook until soft. Add the paprika and cayenne pepper, if using, and cook for a few seconds, then throw in the mussels, passata and white wine and place the lid on the pot. Bring to a boil then reduce to a simmer and cook for just a couple of minutes until all the shells open. Stir through the parsley and some black pepper, then ladle into bowls and serve with crusty bread.

 My mate John Susman, a seafood expert, insists it's an old wives' tale that you can't eat those mussels that don't open when cooked. I would err on the side of caution, though . . .

JAMBALAYA

Serves 4

This is an unashamedly Aussie-fied version of the New Orleans classic, because we can't get the same tasso (smoked ham) or andouille (smoked pork sausage) that they use over there. It's a great one-pot dish, and don't think that I'm being cheap using margarine – it's what's used in traditional Creole cooking.

You'll find filé powder in specialist delis and spice stores.

12 green (raw) king prawns (optional)

50 g margarine

150 g smoked ham, diced

2 smoked pork sausages, sliced

2 chicken thigh fillets, cut into bite-sized pieces

1 large brown onion, finely diced

2 stalks celery, finely sliced

1 large green capsicum, white insides and seeds
    removed, finely diced

2 cloves garlic, finely chopped

2 cups long-grain rice

4 cups Homemade Chicken Stock (see page 208)

SEASONING

2 bay leaves

1 teaspoon sea salt

1 teaspoon white pepper

1 teaspoon cayenne pepper

1 teaspoon filé powder (optional)

½ teaspoon dried thyme leaves

½ teaspoon cumin

½ teaspoon freshly ground black pepper

Prepare the seasoning by mixing all the ingredients together. If you're using prawns, prepare them by twisting off the head and peeling off the shell, leaving the last section of the tail on. Remove the dark intestinal tract.

Melt the margarine in a large, heavy-based pan, then add the ham, sausage and chicken. Cook over medium heat for 5 minutes, stirring occasionally, before adding the onion, celery, capsicum, garlic and seasoning, then cook for a few minutes until the vegetables are soft. Add the rice and stir through, then add the stock. Bring to a boil, then simmer until the rice is al dente and the chicken is cooked through (12–15 minutes). If using prawns, add them about 3 minutes before the end of the cooking time.

BEEF AND GUINNESS PIES

Serves 4

What is it with guys and pies? This version receives similar accolades to the chicken pie (see page 40), but what makes this one perfect for eating in front of the footy (besides the fact there's beer in it) is that you can make the filling the day before and it will taste even better. Then just before the game starts, whack a sheet of puff pastry on top of the filling, throw it into the oven until the pastry browns, and you're done.

1.2 kg beef cheeks or any other beef suitable for
    slow-braising, like chuck or topside, trimmed
    of fat and cut into 2 cm chunks
⅓ cup plain flour
2 tablespoons olive oil
1 large brown onion, chopped *or* 8 pickling onions,
    peeled and halved
1 clove garlic, finely chopped
50 g pancetta *or* bacon, finely sliced
2 stalks celery, sliced
2 carrots, sliced
sea salt and freshly ground black pepper
1 cup ready-made beef or veal stock
    diluted with 1 cup water
1 tablespoon Worcestershire sauce
400 ml Guinness
1 teaspoon thyme leaves
2 bay leaves
1 tablespoon finely chopped flat-leaf parsley
4 sheets frozen puff pastry, thawed
1 organic or free-range egg, beaten with
    a few drops of milk

Preheat the oven to 150°C. Dust the beef chunks in 3 tablespoons of the flour.

Heat the oil in an ovenproof casserole dish and brown the meat, then add the onion, garlic and pancetta or bacon and cook over high heat until lightly browned. Add the celery and carrot and mix through. Add the remaining tablespoon of flour and some salt and pepper, and cook for a minute or so, stirring until the flour has been incorporated. Add the stock, Worcestershire sauce, Guinness and the herbs and stir to combine. Place the lid on the dish, bring the contents to a boil, then carefully transfer the dish to the oven and cook for 2 hours.

Remove from the oven and fish out the bay leaves with a slotted spoon. If making the pies the following day, leave the casserole to cool before storing in the fridge overnight.

The next day, preheat the oven to 200°C and remove the casserole dish from the fridge. Take four small ovenproof pie dishes and cut a piece of thawed puff pastry to cover the top of each dish, trimming it so it hangs over the sides of the dish by about 1 cm. Spoon a quarter of the filling into each dish, place the pastry on top, and pinch the edges together to seal. Pierce the middle of each pastry lid with a knife to allow the steam to escape, and brush the pastry with the egg and milk mixture (this gives it a nice, shiny surface). Bake until the pastry is golden brown, about 15–20 minutes.

 On the subject of pies, the best tip I can give anyone is to never, ever eat the pies at a postponed race meeting.

LAMB SHANKS WITH TOMATOES, OREGANO AND CANNELLINI BEANS

Serves 4 very hungry blokes

This is a feed! With the combination of lamb shanks and white beans, you won't be running any marathons afterwards, but you'll be too busy watching sport on TV anyway. Let it cook for ages then leave it to stand for a little while once you've taken it out of the oven, and this dish will redefine 'hearty' for your mates.

350 g dried cannellini beans
8 lamb shanks
sea salt and freshly ground black pepper
½ cup olive oil
2 leeks, white part only, sliced or 2 brown onions, sliced
2 stalks celery, sliced
2 cloves garlic, sliced
4 anchovies (optional)
2 × 400 g cans tomatoes
1 cup dry white wine
1 piece lemon peel, about 2 cm × 3 cm, white
    pith removed
2 tablespoons fresh oregano leaves
about 24 black olives

Place the cannellini beans in a large bowl and cover with water. Soak for at least 6 hours, or overnight if possible.

Preheat the oven to 150°C. Season the lamb shanks with salt and pepper. Heat half the olive oil in a large heavy-based casserole dish, and brown the shanks in batches, then set them aside. Heat the remaining oil, then add the leeks, celery, garlic and the anchovies, if using, and cook until the vegetables are soft. Return the lamb to the pot and add the cannellini beans, tomatoes, white wine, lemon peel and oregano, and just enough water to cover the ingredients. Pop the lid on and bring the contents to a boil, then transfer the dish to the oven.

After 1 hour, check that there is still plenty of liquid (add some water if it is drying out) and that it is simmering, not boiling rapidly (if the latter, turn the oven temperature down slightly). Cook for a further half an hour to an hour, or until the meat is really tender. Remove from the oven and take out the lemon peel, then stir through the black olives and set aside to rest for 20 minutes. Serve in large, shallow bowls.

SALT-AND-PEPPER SQUID OR PRAWNS

Serves 4 as a snack

This is the perfect half-time snack – and it'll be the best feed your mates have ever had. Prepare your dipping sauce and seafood in advance, then at half-time all you need do is throw together your batter and fry these little beauties up.

4 whole small/medium squid, cleaned
    (ask your fishmonger to do this for you) *or*
    8–12 green (raw) king prawns
1 tablespoon sea salt
1 cup potato flour (available from Asian delis)
½ tablespoon ground Sichuan pepper
½ teaspoon five-spice powder
1 egg white
1 cup neutral oil (see page 6)

DIPPING SAUCE
⅓ cup lemon juice
2 teaspoons white pepper
1 teaspoon kitchen salt

Mix the dipping sauce ingredients together and store in the fridge until required.

Cut the squid tubes in half lengthways and score the outer side in a criss-cross pattern, then cut into bite-sized pieces. Alternatively, if using prawns, prepare by twisting off the head and peeling off the shell, leaving the last section of the tail on. With a sharp knife, cut almost all the way through the back of the prawns so they 'butterfly' out and lie flat, and remove the dark intestinal tract.

Combine the sea salt, potato flour, Sichuan pepper and five-spice in a bowl. In another bowl, beat the egg white until soft peaks form. One by one, dip the squid pieces or prawns in the egg white then the spice mixture to coat.

Heat the oil in a large pan or wok, fry the squid pieces or prawns in batches until golden brown, then drain on paper towel. Serve immediately with the dipping sauce alongside.

BLUE SWIMMER CRABS STIR-FRIED WITH GINGER, LEMONGRASS AND KAFFIR LIME

Serves 4

This is a much lighter, more aromatic alternative to traditional chilli crab or prawns doused in chilli sauce, tomato sauce and cornflour. It might be light and aromatic (blah blah blah) but we're still talking crabs, and crabs are bloke food – get your mates to wear daggy old shirts (advice probably not required) and expect to make a mess; there's no polite way to eat a crab.

2 tablespoons neutral oil (see page 6)
6 raw blue swimmer crabs, cleaned and
    cut into 6 pieces, claws cracked
2 sticks lemongrass, thick end only, thinly sliced
2 cloves garlic, thinly sliced
1 knob ginger (about 3 cm long), peeled
    and thinly sliced
10 kaffir lime leaves, thinly sliced
1 medium-sized red chilli, seeds removed,
    thinly sliced, or more to taste
1 teaspoon sea salt
½ teaspoon sugar
boiled rice or sliced baguette, to serve

Heat a large wok over high heat and add the oil. When the oil is hot, add the crab pieces, lemongrass, garlic, ginger, lime leaves and chilli. Stir well to coat the crab with the other ingredients and to prevent anything from burning.

Add ½ cup water, the salt and sugar, cover with a lid and cook for 3–4 minutes, shaking the wok occasionally to make sure the crab pieces cook evenly. Once cooked, serve immediately in shallow bowls, and spoon the juices over. Serve with boiled rice or baguette slices.

Blue swimmer crabs
stir-fried with ginger,
lemongrass and kaffir lime

OSSO BUCO RISOTTO

Serves 4

I was going to just include the recipe for osso buco, that classic Italian veal-shank dish, but if you make much more than you need, a risotto made from the leftovers is a joy to behold.

Enjoy the osso buco with polenta, spuds or even risotto Milanese (a basic risotto with saffron) with your freeloading mates one night, and back it up a couple of nights later with this unique risotto, partnered with a green salad and plenty of very good red wine.

OSSO BUCO

14 slices of veal shank (shin), about 3 cm thick

1 cup plain flour, seasoned with 1 teaspoon sea salt

½ cup olive oil

4 brown onions, finely chopped

4 cloves garlic, finely chopped

3 carrots, finely chopped

2 stalks celery, finely chopped

1 × 400 g can tomatoes

2 bay leaves

2 cups dry white wine

200 ml marsala (optional)

100 ml ready-made veal stock diluted with 100 ml
   water *or* 200 ml Homemade Chicken Stock
   (see page 208)

1 tablespoon balsamic vinegar

1 tablespoon chopped marjoram

2 tablespoons chopped flat-leaf parsley

RISOTTO

100 g butter

½ brown onion or leek, finely chopped

1¼ cups arborio, vialone or carnaroli rice

½ cup freshly grated parmesan cheese

1 tablespoon flat-leaf parsley, chopped

1 tablespoon marjoram, chopped

To make the osso buco, preheat the oven to 150°C. Dust each piece of veal in the seasoned flour, then heat half the olive oil in a large, heavy-based casserole dish, brown the meat in batches and reserve.

Heat the remaining oil in the casserole dish and soften the onion, garlic, carrot and celery for a few minutes until they start to caramelise. Add the rest of the ingredients, pop the lid on, bring to a boil, then cook in the oven for 2 hours. Serve up to your chums watching the footy, giving them two slices of meat each – much more than they deserve. Leave the leftover osso buco to cool (put it in the fridge and use within a day or so).

To make the risotto, remove the veal from the bones and shred the meat with a sharp knife, discarding any fat or skin. Return the shredded meat to the sauce, and reheat until hot (this sauce is now your stock for the risotto).

In a large, heavy-based saucepan, soften the onion or leek in half the butter, then add the rice. Cook for 1 minute and stir well to coat the rice in butter. Add 1 cup of osso buco sauce and simmer while stirring it through the rice. Keep adding more sauce as the rice absorbs it, about ½ cup at a time, for about 16–18 minutes, by which time the rice should be al dente. Make sure that the final result is wet and soupy, not too firm, by adding a little extra sauce or water if necessary.

Remove from the heat and stir through the remaining butter, the parmesan and the herbs, and serve.

 Browning the shanks in olive oil should leave a nice nut-brown residue in the pan, but if it's blackened and burnt instead, wipe the pan clean before cooking the veg.

LAMB TAGINE

Serves 4–6

Tagines can be flash dinner-party food, a slow braise reheated on a school night, or something to spoil your mates with while watching the footy or cricket. They are another dish that there are seemingly endless variations on, but they always include spices and fruit of some sort added to the meat braise.

You can be extra smart and buy a terracotta tagine (the cooking pot that shares its name with the dish), though it cooks perfectly well in a normal casserole dish.

½ teaspoon sea salt

2 tablespoons plain flour

½ teaspoon sweet paprika

½ teaspoon freshly ground black pepper

1 kg diced lamb shoulder or leg

olive oil, for cooking

2 cloves garlic, chopped

2 large brown onions, finely diced

2 potatoes, peeled and cut into quarters

½ cup blanched almonds

1 tablespoon chopped preserved lemon rind
   (preserved lemons are available from good delis)

½ cup currants

½ teaspoon saffron threads

1 teaspoon ground ginger

1 teaspoon white pepper

pinch cayenne pepper

1 tablespoon honey

1 cup Homemade Chicken Stock (see page 208)
   or ½ cup ready-made chicken stock diluted
   with ½ cup water

8 fresh dates

12 green beans, cut into 4 cm lengths

juice of one lemon

½ cup each coriander and flat-leaf
   parsley leaves, to garnish

steamed couscous, to serve

Mix the salt, flour, paprika and pepper together in a bowl and coat the lamb pieces in this seasoning. Heat some oil in a pan and brown the lamb in batches, then remove and set aside.

In a large, heavy-based casserole dish, soften the garlic and onion in oil. Add the potato, almonds, preserved lemon rind, currants, saffron, ginger, white pepper, cayenne and honey and cook for about a minute. Add the browned lamb, the stock and enough water to cover the ingredients, bring to a boil and simmer for 1¼ hours. Add the dates and beans and simmer for another 5 minutes.

Stir through the lemon juice just before serving, and top with the fresh herbs. Serve with steamed couscous.

Hangover
food

Hangover food

Gentlemen, I assure you that I am qualified to speak on this subject. Unfortunately, I am probably over-qualified.

There are two ways to approach the delicate task of feeding a hangover. The crafty way (for a premeditated hangover, when you're having a big dinner at home and know it's going to be a monster) is to cook more than you need so that you have leftovers for the next day. Genius! I always make plenty of extra frittata, rissoles and fishcakes – for some reason, these really hit the spot the next day when you've got a crushing hangover (along with the appropriate refreshment, of course: I'm a chocolate-flavoured milk kind of guy, not a Coke kind of guy, so I grab some while shopping and fight my eight-year-old daughter for it in the morning).

The second, much tougher way to face a hangover is when the bastard sneaks up on you – there's nothing prepared in the fridge and you have to start from scratch. In this case, my strong recommendation is to head out for yum cha or a greasy fry-up. However, if you feel like you have ice picks through both eyes and are too crook to leave the house (and let's face it, we've all been there), you'll need to cook something as extreme as the way you feel. My personal favourites are disgustingly rich baked eggs with fried onions, or just-plain-silly hotcakes with bacon and maple syrup.

But we all know, deep down, that food is just window-dressing when it comes to fighting hangovers. Fry-ups, reheated leftovers, Panadol, Berocca, litres of water and flavoured milk are all futile in the face of a giant hangover. We might as well accept the fact that we're history until the next morning, and cop it sweet.

'There are two ways to approach the delicate task of feeding a hangover.'

BEEF AND BEETROOT RISSOLES

Serves 4 with lots of leftovers

This is my simplified, much more downmarket version of a dish that renowned chef Mogens Bay Esbensen taught me years ago, and it has become a family staple. It's one to cook for dinner the night before, making sure there are plenty left over, so that when you wake up the next morning with a rude hangover you can crawl straight to the fridge and grab one (or ten).

Canned beetroot is fine for this (it's for an anticipated hangover, not entertaining royalty). And we Aussies love our beetroot – what's a real hamburger without it? You can always beat an egg, but you can't beet-a-root (boom, tish).

butter, for cooking
1 brown or red onion, finely chopped
1 kg premium beef mince
½ × 425 g can sliced beetroot, drained and
    very finely diced
1 tablespoon capers, rinsed and finely chopped
    (choose the ones preserved in salt rather
    than brine if you can find them)
4 egg yolks, from organic or free-range eggs
sea salt and freshly ground black pepper, to taste
neutral oil (see page 6), for frying

DIPPING SAUCE
1 × 300 ml carton sour light cream
2 tablespoons chopped dill
1 tablespoon lemon juice
½ teaspoon freshly ground black pepper

To make the dipping sauce, mix all the ingredients together and store in the fridge until needed.

Melt the butter in a pan, add the onion and cook until soft (don't allow it to brown). Remove from the heat and set aside to cool.

In a large bowl, thoroughly mix the mince, beetroot, capers, egg yolks and cooked onion together with your hands. Season well with salt and pepper, then divide the mixture into golf-ball-sized rissoles.

Heat the oil in a heavy-based frying pan and fry the rissoles in batches, then drain on paper towel and serve immediately with the dipping sauce.

BAKED EGGS WITH ONION CREAM SAUCE

Serves 4

You can make this from scratch when you wake up crook, or, if you are really certain you're going to tie one on, cook it the night before and reheat it in the morning. While the egg and onion combination doesn't necessarily make you pleasant to be around, it's a seriously rich, disgustingly filling and very yummy dish.

About once a year for this one does it for me.

8 organic or free-range eggs
50 g butter
3 medium-sized brown onions, finely sliced
1 tablespoon plain flour
pinch of nutmeg
1 tablespoon finely chopped flat-leaf parsley
sea salt and freshly ground black pepper
1 cup milk
1 cup fresh or packaged breadcrumbs
sourdough toast, to serve

Preheat the oven to 220°C. Put the eggs in a large saucepan filled with cold water, bring to a boil and cook for 5 minutes. Drain immediately and rinse under cold water, then peel the eggs while they are still warm.

Melt the butter in a large frying pan, then cook the onions until just light brown (but don't let them caramelise – an occasional spoonful of water added can help prevent this). Add the flour, nutmeg, parsley and plenty of salt and pepper, and cook, stirring, for about a minute or so. Once all the flour has been incorporated, start adding the milk gradually, stirring constantly to make a thin white sauce (about the consistency of pouring gravy – you may need slightly more or less milk than specified).

Cut the eggs in half and arrange them cut-side up in a ceramic dish big enough to hold the eggs in one layer. Pour the white sauce over the eggs and spread to the edges. Sprinkle the breadcrumbs on top in an even layer, then place the dish in the top part of the oven and cook until the breadcrumbs are browned.

Serve with sourdough toast and the hair of the dog.

CARAMELISED ONION AND ROSEMARY FRITTATA

Serves 4 (but keep as much as you can for the next morning)

The frittata is a tried and tested balm for a giant hangover – all those eggs and salt have a remarkably restorative effect. This is such a lovely simple dish, with the sweet richness of the onions enhanced by the rosemary; it's almost too good to waste on a hangover. Almost.

50 g butter
3 large brown onions, sliced
1 tablespoon chopped rosemary
1 teaspoon balsamic vinegar
8 organic or free-range eggs
2 tablespoons finely grated parmesan cheese
sea salt and freshly ground black pepper
a good glug of olive oil and a bit of extra butter, for cooking

Melt the butter in a non-stick frying pan (about 20 cm wide), add the onions and rosemary and cook until the onions are sweet and brown (about 15 minutes), then add the balsamic vinegar and remove from the heat.

Lightly beat the eggs, then add the parmesan and some salt and pepper. Add the cooked onions to the egg mixture and stir through. Wipe the frying pan clean with paper towel, return to the heat and add the oil and extra butter. Pour in the egg and onion mixture and cook over low heat until the egg is completely set. (You may need to place a lid or some foil over the pan to help cook the top of the eggs quickly if the bottom is browning too much.)

Leave to cool and cut into slices.

If the egg refuses to set, you can either place the pan under a hot grill for just a few seconds, or invert the frittata into another greased pan and cook the top. This last move has a 9.8 degree of difficulty.

BLUEBERRY HOTCAKES WITH BACON AND MAPLE SYRUP

Makes about 10 hotcakes

OK, I know it sounds disgusting, but you're hardly going to have it every morning. And it *is* delicious – in a disgusting sort of way. Blame the Americans; they're always putting sweet and salty things together.

You can substitute cooked fresh corn or raspberries for the blueberries, or leave the hotcakes mercifully plain if you're really feeling crook.

120 g plain flour, sifted
150 ml milk
1 heaped teaspoon baking powder
3 organic or free-range eggs, separated
1 punnet fresh blueberries *or* 300 g frozen blueberries
10 bacon rashers
butter, for cooking
real maple syrup (not the flavoured stuff) to serve, plus extra butter if you must

Turn the oven on to its lowest setting.

Add the flour, milk and baking powder to the egg yolks and mix to a thick batter. Beat the whites until stiff and gently fold them through the batter, then fold in the blueberries.

Put the bacon rashers on to grill. Melt a little butter in a small, non-stick pan, and add a ladleful of batter to the pan. Cook for a minute or two until small bubbles form on the edge of the hotcake, flip it over and cook the other side for another minute or so, then transfer the hotcake to the oven to keep warm while you cook the rest.

To serve, top the hotcakes with a rasher of grilled bacon and plenty of maple syrup.

If you're breaking eggs into a bowl and a piece of shell falls in, you could chase it around forever with a spoon. But use half an eggshell to scoop it out, and the relcalcitrant piece virtually jumps straight in.

Blueberry hotcakes with bacon and maple syrup

TRADITIONAL ENGLISH FISHCAKES WITH TARTARE SAUCE

Serves 4, or 2 with lots of leftovers

Here's another dish that would be just as appropriate at a 'noice' dinner party or to feed the family as it is for providing hangover relief. This recipe looks pretty unremarkable; there's nothing very special about the ingredients. But cook it once and it will be one of those recipes that you cook all the time. The leftovers ain't half bad, either.

400 g blue-eye or other flaky white fish
1 large desiree or other waxy potato
2½ cups packaged breadcrumbs
¼ cup chopped flat-leaf parsley
2 tablespoons finely grated parmesan cheese
1 clove garlic, crushed
2 organic or free-range eggs, beaten
sea salt and white pepper
1 cup plain flour
1 teaspoon sea salt
2 organic or free-range eggs, beaten with
    a tablespoon of cold water (eggwash)
neutral oil (see page 6), for frying

TARTARE SAUCE
1 cup Homemade Mayonnaise (see page 208)
    or good quality ready-made mayonnaise
2 tablespoons finely chopped cornichons *or* dill pickles
1 tablespoon stuffed olives, chopped
1 tablespoon grated white onion *or* golden shallot
1 tablespoon capers, chopped
1 tablespoon chopped flat-leaf parsley
1 tablespoon lemon juice

To make the tartare sauce, simply mix all the ingredients together and store in an airtight container in the fridge.

In a shallow heavy-based pan, heat 3 cups of salted water to simmering point (do not boil). Add the fish and poach for about 10–15 minutes, or until cooked through. Remove from the pan and drain on paper towel, then flake the fish with a fork.

Bring a pan of salted water to a boil and cook the potato until just tender, then mash and leave to cool.

In a large bowl, combine the fish, potato, 1 cup of the breadcrumbs, parsley, parmesan cheese, garlic, egg, salt and pepper, and then shape carefully into 8 neat patties. Chill these in the fridge for 30 minutes to firm them up.

Arrange three small plates in front of you. Put the plain flour and salt in one, the eggwash in the second, and the rest of the breadcrumbs in the third. Take each fishcake and dip it in the flour, then the eggwash before thoroughly coating with the breadcrumbs.

Fry the fishcakes in the oil on medium–high heat until golden brown, and serve with the tartare sauce on the side.

THE TERAKES
BREAKFAST FRY-UP
Serves 1

You hardly need a recipe for a fry-up, but this version is one I resort to at home when necessary. One egg and a rasher of that stupid bacon without any fat on it (Homer Simpson would be rightly outraged) will simply not do. If you're going to have a fry-up, do it properly and make plenty of it. Fried eggs, nice and runny, are an alternative, but scrambled nicely matches your addled brain.

This version feeds one hungover bloke, but just multiply everything by four to feed a group of hungover blokes (multiplication might make your head hurt, though).

1 thin beef sausage
2–3 rashers bacon
1 large ripe tomato, halved
2 thick slices multigrain or sourdough bread
3 large organic or free-range eggs
4 tablespoons cream
sea salt and freshly ground black pepper
25 g butter

Put the sausage, bacon and tomato on to grill, or fry them in a large frying pan.

Pop the bread in the toaster, then beat the eggs with 2 tablespoons of the cream and a large pinch of salt and pepper. In a non-stick pan, melt the butter and add the rest of the cream, then pour in the egg mixture, cooking over a medium heat and stirring constantly until just set.

Spoon the eggs onto the buttered toast with the banger, bacon and tomato, and serve with a fresh orange juice, strong coffee and headache pills.

PORK FILLET SCHNITZEL
WITH COLESLAW
Serves 4, with some leftovers

Leftover crumbed fried things won't grace too many flash restaurant menus, but thin slices of fried crumbed pork sprinkled liberally with sea salt are manna from heaven when you feel like there's an ice pick in one or both eyes. Strangely enough, this is quite a delicious dish served hot, too.

¼ cabbage, very finely sliced, thick stalk removed
2 stalks celery, sliced
2 carrots, grated
1 small red onion, finely sliced
½ cup sultanas
1 tablespoon grain mustard
juice of ½ lemon
½ cup chopped flat-leaf parsley
1–1½ cups Homemade Mayonnaise (see page 208)
  or good quality ready-made mayonnaise
1 cup plain flour, seasoned with 1 teaspoon salt
2 organic or free-range eggs
2 cups packaged breadcrumbs
2 large pork fillets, diagonally sliced into discs
  and flattened
about 2 cups neutral oil (see page 6)
1 lemon, cut into quarters, to garnish
boiled new potatoes, to serve

To make the coleslaw, combine the cabbage, celery, carrot and onion in a large bowl. Add the sultanas, mustard, lemon juice, parsley and enough mayo to coat the vegetables without making the salad too gluggy.

For the schnitzels, arrange three bowls in front of you. Add the flour and the salt to one, the beaten egg and a tablespoon of water to the second, and the breadcrumbs to the third.

Take each piece of pork and dip it in the flour then the egg before thoroughly coating with the breadcrumbs. Heat the oil in a large, shallow frying pan and fry the schnitzels until golden brown, turning them once.

Serve the schnitzels garnished with a lemon quarter, and boiled new potatoes on the side.

 If you have one, use a meat mallet to flatten the fillets, or the base of your fist will do.

Pork fillet schnitzel
with coleslaw

LEFTOVER
SPAG-BOL FRITTATA
Serves 4

You can always cheat a bit with frittata
and add some of last night's dinner as your
filling – it is one of the great leftover food
groups. It's worth making some extra spag
bol to be able to whip up this frittata the next
morning. You'll need to be a bit heavy-handed
with the salt, pepper and parmesan here
though, because pasta can tend to be a bit
bland in a frittata.

8 organic or free-range eggs
½ cup finely grated parmesan cheese
½ cup chopped flat-leaf parsley
sea salt and freshly ground black pepper
2 cups leftover Spag Bol (see page 188)
olive oil and butter, for cooking

Lightly beat the eggs, then add the parmesan, parsley,
salt and pepper and fold through the leftover spag bol.
    Melt the butter and oil in a deep, non-stick frying pan.
Pour the egg mixture into the pan and turn the heat
to low. Cook until the egg is completely set (you may
need to place a lid or some foil over the pan to help
cook the top of the eggs quickly if the bottom is
browning too much).
    Leave to cool, then slice into wedges and serve.

STIR-FRIED PORK WITH BEAN
SAUCE AND FRESH HERBS
Serves 2 with leftovers

This is another recipe that's evolved over time.
It was originally a Ken Hom dish, combining
king prawns with what seemed like way too
many fresh herbs (but never was) and Chinese
bean sauce, which is one of the squillion fabulous things you can find in Asian supermarkets
for a dollar or so.
    In the Terakes household, the recipe was
adapted by substituting thinly sliced pork fillet
or pork mince for the prawns, and by adding
some asparagus for a contrasting, slightly
crunchy texture. I serve it with steamed rice as
a standard school-night meal because it's so
quick and easy to cook. But I deliberately make
too much, because the saltiness of the bean
sauce makes it delicious cold the next day
(though it's even better after half an hour out
of the fridge, if you can wait that long).

1 tablespoon neutral oil (see page 6)
500–750 g pork fillet, finely sliced or 500–750 g pork
    mince from an Asian butcher (this makes plenty
    of leftovers)
2 tablespoons bean paste, often called bean sauce
1 bunch asparagus, woody ends trimmed and discarded,
    cut into 1 cm pieces
1 cup basil leaves, finely sliced
1 cup coriander leaves, roughly chopped
1 cup flat-leaf parsley leaves, roughly chopped
6 spring onions, white part only, finely chopped
boiled rice, to serve

Heat a large wok, add the oil, then stir-fry the pork until
just brown. Pile in all the other ingredients and stir-fry
until the meat is cooked. Transfer to a large bowl and
serve with boiled rice.

ROAST RIB EYE WITH CARROT 'JAM'

Serves 4

This is not for the faint-hearted. You can roast a whole sirloin or even a fillet, but the principle is the same – if you brown the meat really well, cook it to medium–rare then let it rest, it will be succulent and tender every time. Partner it with the delicious gratin opposite, and you'll have the perfect meal, plus the perfect hangover cure with the leftovers.

Veal glaze is available from most good butchers, delis and food halls of big department stores.

1 whole beef rib eye, also known as standing
    rib roast (allow one rib per person)
olive oil, for rubbing
sea salt
50 g butter
1 white onion, finely sliced
2 carrots, coarsely grated
2 tablespoons roughly chopped rosemary leaves
1 tablespoon freshly ground black pepper
3 tablespoons honey
1 tablespoon veal glaze
Potato and Parmesan Gratin, to serve

Preheat the oven to 180°C. Rub the beef all over with the olive oil and season well with sea salt. Heat a large frying pan to searing, and quickly brown the outside of the meat well (the idea is to caramelise the skin without cooking it too much). Place the meat in a large baking dish, transfer to the oven and cook for about 1 hour, or until medium–rare (the exact cooking time will depend on the size of the roast). Once cooked, remove the meat from the oven and set aside to rest for 15 minutes, loosely covered with foil.

Meanwhile, melt the butter in a saucepan and cook the onion, carrot and rosemary until just soft. Add the pepper and honey and reduce the heat to low. Simmer for about 30 minutes, until the mixture has reduced to a soft, jammy consistency, and set aside.

Transfer the meat to a chopping board and drain the fat from the roasting pan, leaving a few tablespoons of the meat juices. Add the veal glaze to the juices and heat, stirring to incorporate, until the sauce is hot.

Slice the meat, giving each person a rib. Spoon over some sauce and top with a spoonful of carrot jam. Serve with Potato and Parmesan Gratin.

POTATO AND PARMESAN GRATIN

Serves 4

'Doctor, doctor, I can feel my arteries clogging.' You won't find this one in any diet books. How good is it, though? It's disgustingly rich and creamy (in fact, with its cream, cheese, potatoes and salt, it's the ultimate hangover food – these are all the food groups necessary when you're at death's door).

150 g butter
4 large desiree or other waxy potatoes,
    peeled and cut into slices about 3 mm thick
1 cup freshly grated parmesan cheese
2 tablespoons chopped rosemary or thyme leaves
sea salt and freshly ground black pepper
1 cup pouring cream

Preheat the oven to 180°C and grease a small baking dish.

Melt the butter in a large frying pan and gently fry the potatoes until half-cooked. Fill the baking dish with layers of potato slices, parmesan cheese, herbs and salt and pepper, finishing with a sprinkling of parmesan. Pour the cream over.

Bake for about 20 minutes, until the potato is cooked through and the top is golden brown.

HOT GINGERBREAD CAKE WITH CARAMEL SAUCE

Serves 6

Sydney chef Mark Armstrong made this dessert flavour-of-the-month back in the late eighties, and it became one of the most-copied desserts in Sydney bistros and brasseries for years.

Re-run the dessert, including the ice cream, with some strong black coffee the morning after the night before, and while it probably won't fix your hangover, you will have had something yummy to eat.

2½ cups plain flour
2 teaspoons ground ginger
1½ teaspoons ground cinnamon
½ teaspoon ground nutmeg
½ teaspoon baking powder
3 teaspoons bicarbonate of soda
½ teaspoon ground cloves
3 organic or free-range eggs
¾ cup brown sugar
¾ cup golden syrup
150 g melted butter
1 cup boiling water
vanilla ice cream, to serve

CARAMEL SAUCE
1 cup sugar
½–1 cup cream

Preheat the oven to 180°C and line a small baking dish with non-stick baking paper. Sift the flour, ginger, cinnamon, nutmeg, baking powder, bicarbonate of soda and cloves together. In a large bowl, whisk the eggs, then add the sugar, golden syrup and melted butter and combine. Add the dry ingredients, pour over the boiling water and mix well. Transfer to the baking dish and bake for 30 minutes.

To make the caramel sauce, dissolve the sugar in 2 tablespoons of water in a saucepan over medium heat. Cook until the sauce turns golden (don't let it turn really dark brown), then add the cream, stirring constantly, and cook for just a minute or two, until it is the consistency of a pouring sauce.

Serve a piece of the cake with a scoop of vanilla ice cream and top with the warm sauce.

Food to seduce

Food to seduce

In my cooking classes these recipes have been ungraciously named 'a route to a root', a phrase coined not only by the blokes but also by the surprising number of women who attend – equally interested, it seems, in gleaning the secrets of seduction.

When planning the menu for a romantic night in, think logically. If the goal is to finish up in the sack and have a good time when you get there, common sense should be your guide. Let's start with drinks. Think Champagne – from France, not sparkling wine. And the better it is, the better it generally is, if you get my drift. On the other hand, some swear by martinis. There's no denying they're elegant, but they're lethal and they numb your palate (of course, if you're a dud cook, by all means administer four quickly and you'll both forget about dinner).

Now, what to eat? Politeness suggests that it's worth finding out what your date does and doesn't like, food-wise. You might enjoy raw fish, offal or a rare beef fillet, but they might not (it's also worth spelling out that your famous steak tartare is raw, to save them resorting to stuffing it in their pockets, Mr Bean-style). Secondly, don't serve anything that makes your breath stink. Parmigiano Reggiano is one of the wonders of the culinary world, but lovely big chunks of it give you bad breath, so it's on the banned list, along with raw garlic or onions. Farting might be hysterically funny when the boys are around for the big game, but it doesn't add much to your seduction technique, so skip the pulses, cabbage and boiled eggs as well.

Your idea of a good time might be a 700 g T-bone steak, but it will sit in your stomach like a bowling ball and is therefore not conducive to hanky panky. Nor is a jungle curry that will get you sweating like pigs before you want to be. And I love chilli crab as much as anyone, but it's messy. You're likely to get it all over you and look like a loser, while your date's a chance to get a drop on their new silk Fendi shirt, ruining their mood along with your chances. (Then again, you might be in the company of someone who enjoys getting food all over themselves, so dust off that old *9½ Weeks* video and start with the sticky pork ribs.)

So, what *can* you serve? Show-off stuff. Make a risotto and share a drink by the stove while you stir it – you caring, clever thing, you. But don't be too clever and plan an eight-course banquet; if you get as far as the seventh course, you probably won't be getting anywhere else. The truth is, no matter what you cook, your date will be impressed and grateful. Hopefully, very grateful.

'Your idea of a good time might be a 700 g T-bone steak, but it will sit in your stomach like a bowling ball and is therefore not conducive to hanky panky.'

Lobster, peach and basil salad (see page 81)

SMOKED-SALMON-BUTTER CANAPÉS
Makes 12 canapés

These are delicious little mouthfuls of sweet butter and salty smoked salmon on crunchy Melba toast squares. They are elegant and subtle – just like your seduction technique, hopefully.

100 g butter, softened
50 g smoked salmon, very finely chopped
1 teaspoon very finely sliced chives or dill
pinch white pepper
a few drops lemon juice

TO SERVE
½ packet Melba toast squares

Simply mix all the ingredients in a bowl and spread on the toast squares.

RAW SALMON WITH PICKLED GINGER AND CAPERS
Makes 12 canapés

Just a mouthful, but these are a fabulous contrasting combination of flavours. It's a good idea to always have some pickled ginger and capers in your fridge, then all you need do is buy a small piece of sashimi-grade salmon from your fishmonger and you can rustle up a quick canapé anytime.

12 very thin slices (across the fillet) sashimi-grade
**   salmon, skin and pin bones removed**
12 small slices pickled ginger
24 small salt-preserved capers, rinsed

Place each piece of salmon flat on a clean surface then place a slice of ginger and two capers at one end. Roll from this end into small tubes and arrange on a serving platter.

WITLOF WITH AVOCADO CREAM AND SALMON EGGS
Makes 12 canapés

A perfect start to that all-important first date. Firstly, these can be eaten with your fingers without making a mess. Secondly, they are delicious – slightly bitter witlof, creamy avocado and salty, rich salmon eggs. And most importantly, they are also quite sexy, with their contrasting crisp, creamy and egg-popping textures.

1 medium-sized witlof
½ ripe avocado
½ teaspoon lemon juice
1 tablespoon cream
1 small jar of salmon eggs (make sure
**   you check the use-by date)**

Cut off the stem of the witlof about 1 cm up and discard. Wash and dry the leaves, discarding the largest and smallest – you should finish up with about eight.
   Press the flesh from the avocado through a very fine sieve and mix it well with the lemon juice and cream.
   Place a small teaspoon of the avocado mixture in the middle of each leaf and pop a teaspoon of salmon eggs on top.

SALAD OF BUFFALO MOZZARELLA, RADICCHIO, PROSCIUTTO AND HONEY

Serves 2

Here's a dish that is lovely and light but full of flavour and texture. The bitter crisp radicchio, the silky salty prosciutto, the creamy mozzarella, the sharpness of the lemon juice, the lovely richness of the olive oil and the surprising burst of honey – you can taste every delicious ingredient.

4–6 radicchio leaves, torn
2 slices prosciutto or jamon, sliced
1 ball buffalo mozzarella cheese, torn into about
    6 or 8 pieces
1 tablespoon extra virgin olive oil
1 teaspoon lemon juice
1 teaspoon finest quality honey
freshly ground black pepper

Arrange the radicchio, prosciutto and mozzarella on two plates. Mix the oil and lemon juice together and sprinkle over the salads, then drizzle with the honey and grind over some black pepper.

LOBSTER, PEACH AND BASIL SALAD

Serves 2

This is simply a beautiful dish, and it's up to you how you wish to serve it.

You could present it as a small but decadent main course following a light entrée, drinking Champagne all the way, or you could reduce the quantities given here for a very flash variation on a shellfish cocktail. But you really must have a very fresh lobster and top quality oil for this one to work.

⅔ cup good quality extra virgin olive oil
3 tablespoons fresh lime juice
1 red shallot *or* ½ small red onion, cut into
    the finest dice possible
sea salt and freshly ground pepper, to taste
1 × 1 kg fresh cooked lobster, meat removed
    from head and tail and cut into 2 cm pieces
2 ripe peaches, preferably freestones, peeled
    and sliced
about 20 basil leaves, roughly torn

Mix the oil, lime juice and shallot or onion in a large bowl and season with salt and pepper. Add the lobster meat, peaches and basil and fold very gently to coat with the dressing, then spoon onto individual plates and serve immediately.

ASPARAGUS RISOTTO

Serves 2 as an entrée

This is a wonderfully versatile dish. It's easy for a school-night meal, or it can be poshed up with some pan-fried prawns for a dinner party. On a hot date, serve a small portion as an entrée, and you can chat around the stove as you lovingly, caringly stir the risotto, being the new-age, 'I can cook' kind of guy that you are.

½ leek, white part only, finely sliced or
   ½ small brown onion, finely chopped
2 tablespoons butter
½–1 bunch asparagus, woody ends discarded,
   finely sliced
½ cup arborio, vialone or carnaroli rice
2 cups Homemade Chicken Stock (see page 208)
1 tablespoon chopped flat-leaf parsley
2 tablespoons finely grated parmesan cheese
sea salt and freshly ground black pepper

In a large, heavy-based saucepan, soften the leek or onion in 1 tablespoon of the butter. Add the asparagus and the rice and stir through so the rice is well coated. Cook for a minute or so, then add 1 cup of stock and simmer while stirring the stock through the rice. Keep adding more stock as the rice absorbs it, about ½ cup at a time, and cook, stirring, for about 16–18 minutes, by which time the rice should be al dente. Make sure that the final result is wet and soupy, not too firm, by adding a little extra stock or water if necessary.

   Remove from the heat and fold in the parsley and parmesan, before stirring through the remaining tablespoon of butter and some salt and pepper.

VEAL FILLET WITH PEAS AND LEEK IN ROSEMARY CREAM

Serves 2

There is a lovely sweetness to this recipe as the peas, leek and cream combine beautifully. Simply pan-fried or roasted in a hot oven, veal fillets are the perfect partner to this sauce. Not every butcher will have them, though, so you may have to trawl through a few before you find them, or order in advance. Lamb fillets or loins will also work well, but the sauce is too sweet for beef.

2 veal fillets, trimmed of fat and sinew
olive oil, for cooking
sea salt
1 small leek, white part only, finely sliced
1 teaspoon butter
1 cup shelled green peas
1 large sprig rosemary, leaves picked
   and finely chopped
100 ml Homemade Chicken Stock (see page 208)
100 ml cream
freshly ground black pepper

Rub the veal with a little olive oil and season well with sea salt. Pan-fry in oil for 10–15 minutes until medium–rare, then leave the cooked meat to rest for 10 minutes. (If roasting, cook for the same time in a 200°C oven, and rest as above.)

   While the veal is cooking, soften the leek in the butter in a saucepan, then add the peas, rosemary and stock. Cover and simmer for 10 minutes. Add the cream and simmer for another 5 minutes uncovered, then season with salt and pepper.

   Slice the veal into thick slices and serve on top of a bed of the peas and leek.

Veal fillet with peas and
leek in rosemary cream

BEEF FILLET AND VICHYSSOISE PURÉE

Serves 2

This is essentially a thicker version of your classic vichyssoise soup paired with a contemporary twist on filet mignon, with a paper-thin slice of prosciutto replacing the thick slice of bacon that dominated the flavour in the old-fashioned version.

Too much of a good thing is the only risk with this dish. Keep the servings small and not too filling, so you're still hungry for lurve.

2 small pieces prime beef eye fillet (3 cm thick)
2 thin slices prosciutto
2 teaspoons butter, plus a tablespoon extra
1 leek, white part only, finely sliced
2 medium-sized desiree or other waxy potatoes,
    peeled and roughly chopped
200–300 ml Homemade Chicken Stock (see page 208)
sea salt and freshly ground black pepper
olive oil, for cooking
1 bunch asparagus
about 12 snowpeas or beans
1 small head broccoli, broken into small florets
2 tablespoons cream
1 teaspoon balsamic vinegar
small bunch chives, cut into 5 cm lengths

Remove the steaks from the fridge about 20 minutes before cooking. Wrap a slice of prosciutto around each of the steaks, securing with a toothpick if necessary, and set aside.

Melt 1 teaspoon of the butter in a small heavy-based saucepan, and add the leeks and potatoes, gently coating them in butter. Cook until the leeks have softened (but do not brown), and add just enough chicken stock to cover. Simmer with the lid on for about 15 minutes, or until the potatoes are cooked. Remove from the heat and purée with a stab blender, making sure all the lumps are removed. Replace the lid and set aside.

Bring a large saucepan of water to a boil for the green vegetables. Season the steaks with plenty of salt and pepper on both sides. Melt a teaspoon of butter and a drizzle of oil in a frying pan, then cook the steaks for a couple of minutes either side, or to your taste. Transfer the steaks to a bowl and leave to rest in a warm place for 5 minutes, reserving the pan to make a sauce later.

Start cooking your green veg in the boiling water now. Asparagus and beans will take about 3 minutes, broccoli about 1 minute and snowpeas about 30 seconds.

Gently reheat the vichysoisse purée (take care not to let it boil) and stir through the cream and a tablespoon of butter to give a silky smooth finish. Spoon a big dollop in the middle of each plate and place a steak on top. Pour the juices from the resting steak and the teaspoon of balsamic vinegar into the frying pan used to cook the steaks and heat, stirring to incorporate any juices left in the bottom of the pan. Spoon this over each steak, top with the chives, and serve the green vegetables alongside.

 For beautiful, browned meat, make sure the frying pan is nice and hot before you add the oil and butter.

GRUYÈRE, CARAWAY AND THYME BREAD AND BUTTER PUDDING

Serves 2

This dish breaks a few food-to-seduce rules because it's a bit on the heavy side, but for some reason it is just about the ultimate 'girl food'. Every girl who tastes it at my cooking classes loves it – and guys can't see what the fuss is about. Serve it with a sharply dressed green salad to cut through the richness of the eggs and cheese.

This recipe makes enough for two, with leftovers for breakfast in bed, if you're so inclined.

½ tablespoon butter, plus more for greasing

½ tablespoon olive oil

1 large brown onion, sliced

½ large baguette, thinly sliced and buttered

1 tablespoon fresh thyme leaves

2 teaspoons caraway seeds

sea salt and freshly ground pepper

200 g gruyère cheese, coarsely grated

3 organic or free-range eggs

350 ml milk

Preheat the oven to 180°C. Grease one medium-sized or two small oval or rectangular baking dishes with a little butter. Melt half a tablespoon of butter with the olive oil in a frying pan, and cook the onions until soft and golden brown – do not let them burn or go crisp.

Add a layer of buttered bread slices to the base of the dish, followed by a sprinkling of thyme, caraway seeds, salt and pepper, and then a layer of onions and a layer of grated cheese. Repeat until all ingredients are used up (you should have two or three complete layers, ending up with onions and cheese on top).

Beat the eggs and milk together and pour carefully into the dish, then bake for 30–40 minutes, until the custard is set and the top is golden brown.

 Don't use fresh white sandwich bread for this one – a crusty baguette (preferably a day or so old) will provide the texture and shape you need.

SALAD OF BEEF FILLET, SOBA NOODLES AND CHOY SUM WITH PONZU DRESSING

Serves 2

This is a very light, clean dish with miles of flavour and some nicely contrasting textures. It's served cold, so all the prepping can be done beforehand and it can be assembled in two minutes when your date arrives.

Ponzu is a Japanese sauce or dressing with a unique citrus character; you can buy it (and mirin) from Japanese food stores and specialist delis.

1 × 125 g slice beef fillet steak
1 tablespoon light soy sauce
¼ teaspoon sesame oil
50 g dried soba noodles
½ bunch choy sum, washed thoroughly
1 tablespoon mirin
2 tablespoons ponzu dressing
1 spring onion, white and pale green parts only, finely sliced
1 teaspoon sesame seeds

Marinate the beef in the soy sauce and sesame oil for 2 hours, covered, in the refrigerator. Bring the beef to room temperature by removing from the fridge half an hour before cooking, and drain off the marinade.

Heat a large wok or frying pan and sear the beef evenly on both sides until just medium–rare. Leave to cool, then refrigerate until ready to serve.

Cook the soba noodles as per the instructions on the pack, and immerse in iced water to cool.

Steam or boil the choy sum for 1 minute only, until just tender, then immerse in iced water immediately to halt the cooking process and maintain colour.

Drain the noodles and the choy sum. Slice the beef thinly and arrange the noodles, choy sum and beef slices on two plates. Combine the mirin and ponzu dressing and spoon over the meat on each plate, then sprinkle with spring onions and sesame seeds and serve immediately.

FETTUCCINE WITH CITRUS ZEST AND SMOKED SALMON

Serves 2

Pasta can be a bit heavy on a hot date, especially with meat sauces. But, as pasta dishes go, this is lighter than most (despite the cream) and certainly very different, with the citrus zest giving the dish a wonderfully fresh character. It probably needs a nice rich chardonnay to wash it down.

200 g dried fettuccine or other thin pasta
100 ml thick cream
100 ml pouring cream
finely grated zest of ½ lemon
finely grated zest of ½ orange
1½ tablespoons brandy
5 mint leaves, finely sliced
50 g smoked salmon, sliced into thin strips
¼ cup freshly grated parmesan cheese

Bring a large saucepan of salted water to a boil, slide in the pasta and cook until al dente.

Meanwhile, place the creams, citrus zest and brandy into a large saucepan, bring to a boil and simmer for 5 minutes.

Drain the pasta well before adding it to the pan with the cream sauce. Fold through the mint, salmon and parmesan and serve immediately.

Fettuccine with citrus zest
and smoked salmon

SALMON WITH
SORREL BUTTER SAUCE

Serves 2

There's something quite sexy about the texture of warm, meltingly tender salmon, and the slight bitterness of the sorrel balances its sweetness nicely. I've included a neat trick to cooking the salmon here so it is velvety tender.

Serve this with mixed salad leaves.

2 brown shallots, finely chopped
1 cup white wine
½ cup white-wine vinegar
2 × 150 g salmon fillets, skin on, pin bones removed
sea salt and freshly ground black pepper
½ bunch sorrel, leaves only, cut into ribbons
100 g cold butter, chopped into chunks

Place the shallots in a small saucepan with the wine and vinegar. Cook over low heat until the liquid has reduced to 3–4 tablespoons. Strain the sauce through a fine sieve into another small saucepan, discarding the solids.

Heat a large non-stick frying pan until hot, then season the salmon with salt and pepper and place it in the dry pan, skin-side down, and cook for 2 minutes. Turn the fish over and cook the other side for about 90 seconds (the centre should still be quite rare). Remove the fish to a warm plate, loosely cover with foil, and let it stand for 5 minutes – the fish will continue to cook and will be perfectly done by the time you're ready to serve.

Bring the reduced sauce to a boil, add the sorrel and stir constantly for about a minute to break up or 'melt' the leaves. Remove from the heat and stir in the butter until melted. Pour the sauce over the salmon fillets and serve.

 The salmon must be at room temperature (not cold) when it goes in the pan, otherwise it won't cook all the way through.

SPAGHETTI MARINARA FRESCO

Serves 2 as a light meal or entrée

Another luxurious dish, but very clean in its flavours – you can distinctly taste the tomatoes, the shellfish and the herbs. Don't be tempted to up the amount of pasta – the generous ratio of seafood to pasta is what makes this dish so special.

You can get away with frozen lobster tails with this one if you can't get fresh, and you could even throw in some chopped fresh scallops or crab meat if you can get your hands on them. If you're serving this as a light meal, follow it up with a generous helping of dessert.

100 g good quality dried spaghetti or spaghettini
¼ cup finest quality extra virgin olive oil
½ clove garlic, crushed
1 red shallot, very finely diced
½ cup (about 150 g) chopped green (raw) prawn meat
½ cup (about 150 g) chopped green (raw) lobster meat
½ cup peeled and diced tomato flesh
½ cup finely chopped mix of basil, chives and
    flat-leaf parsley
sea salt and freshly ground black pepper
crusty bread, to serve

Bring a large saucepan of salted water to a boil, slide in the pasta and cook until al dente.

Meanwhile, heat a third of the oil in a large, heavy-based pan and cook the garlic and shallot until softened. Add the prawn and lobster meat and increase the heat to high. Fold through the tomatoes and simmer for 1–2 minutes.

Drain the pasta and add it to the pan along with the herbs and the remaining oil, and mix through to combine. Season well with salt and pepper and serve immediately.

 To peel a tomato, make an 'x' in the base with a sharp knife, drop into boiling water for 10 seconds then immerse immediately in cold water. The skin should peel off easily.

RASPBERRY SOUFFLÉ
Serves 2

Everyone thinks that soufflés are diabolically difficult – the business of serious-looking men in tall chef's hats. Forget the clichés: they aren't that hard. In fact, I've never had a failure in twenty-plus years of soufflé-ing.

Restaurant soufflés are made with a flour base, which complicates things and increases the degree of difficulty. With my method, you're really only mixing a berry purée with beaten egg whites. But enough of the technical stuff: the bottom line is, if you make a girl a soufflé and it rises, but you still miss out, give up.

butter, for greasing
100 g caster sugar, plus more for dusting
150 g raspberries, plus extra to serve
3 egg whites from organic or free-range eggs

Preheat the oven to 200°C. Lightly grease two small (8 cm) soufflé dishes with butter and dust them with caster sugar, inverting the dishes to tip out any excess before placing on a baking tray.

Purée the raspberries with half the sugar using a stab blender or a food processor. Whisk the egg whites, gradually adding the remaining sugar, until stiff peaks form. Gently fold in the raspberry purée (don't beat it – you want as much air as possible in the soufflé). Fill the dishes with the mixture and bake for about 5 minutes, until they've risen and the tops are brown.

These are perfect just as they are, but you can serve a few fresh raspberries alongside if you like.

 Opening the oven door to check on progress will make for a very flat soufflé. Try cleaning the glass on your oven door instead . . .

POACHED PEACHES IN LEMONGRASS, GINGER AND VANILLA SYRUP

Serves 2

Asian flavours in a dessert might seem unusual, but they add an elegant touch to poached peaches, nicely balancing the sweetness of this dish. Just make sure you buy freestone peaches, the ones where the stone slips away from the flesh easily, or you and the object of your lust will be chasing them around your plates all night.

2 freestone peaches
vanilla or coconut ice cream, to serve

SYRUP
½ vanilla bean, split lengthways
1 stick lemongrass, thick white part only, sliced
2 star anise
½ small knob ginger (about 1.5 cm), peeled and finely sliced
2 tablespoons grated palm sugar

Place all the syrup ingredients in a saucepan and add about ½ litre of water. Bring to a boil, then reduce the heat and simmer for about 15 minutes. Add the whole peaches to the pan (ensuring they are completely covered with the liquid), put the lid on and gently poach over low heat for 5–10 minutes, or until the peaches are just tender. Gently remove the peaches from the syrup and peel them as soon as they're cool enough to handle.

Turn the heat to high and reduce the liquid by more than half until it thickens to a syrup consistency. Remove the syrup from the heat and, when it has cooled completely, lower the peaches back in, cover and refrigerate until use. Serve with vanilla or coconut ice cream.

ZABAGLIONE

Serves 2

Zabaglione is the ultimate seductive dessert. On one hand it is beautifully rich, while on the other it's light and airy after being whisked to within an inch of its life. Invite your friend to share a glass of dessert wine with you while you're whisking away at the stove.

3 egg yolks from organic or free-range eggs
3 tablespoons caster sugar
2 tablespoons marsala
sponge finger biscuits, to serve

Bring a small amount of water to a boil in a saucepan. In a small heatproof bowl that will fit snugly over the saucepan, whisk the egg yolks and sugar together until pale.

Place the bowl over the saucepan of simmering water (don't let the bottom of the bowl touch the water) and continue to whisk, gradually adding the marsala. Keep whisking until the mixture doubles in volume, then serve in cocktail glasses with sponge finger biscuits alongside.

The new Aussie barbecue

The new Aussie barbecue

The great Aussie barbie has come a long way since its modest beginnings in the heady days of the 1960s, and we are now cooking outdoors and enjoying the flavours of grilled food much more often. When I first started my cooking classes, a lot of, shall we say, more traditional blokes said to me that the classes were a fine idea, just not for them – the kitchen was the woman's domain. But if I were to run classes for barbecue cooking – now *that* they could get excited about. So I did.

While it's not rocket science, there are a few basic rules to follow to ensure your barbie is a celebration of tender, succulent meat and flavoursome chargrilled veggies rather than a collection of charcoal morsels, crucified on the outside but still raw in the middle. In my classes, I found that what blokes really wanted to know was how to cook basic steaks and bangers better, as well as learn a few barbie trade secrets they could use to big-note themselves by passing them on to their mates, eg 'Of course, you know that the steak has to be at room temperature to cook evenly, mate, don't you?' Most importantly, though, they wanted a couple of simple, reliable dishes that were a bit special, that they could pull out to impress their mates and that would become their party pieces.

What they didn't much want to know, but found out anyway, were some basic food-hygiene rules, however unsexy they may be. Funnily enough, just turning the hotplate on full blast and giving it a scrape doesn't remove the crap that has built up over the past six months. And guys are astonished to find out that it's not OK to put the cooked meat back onto the plate it came to the barbecue on, or pour leftover marinade over cooked meat without boiling it first.

Of course, for a full run-down on barbecuing in the 21st century, you need to get yourself a copy of my first book, *The Great Aussie Barbie Cookbook*. It's the pigeon-pair to this one and, according to my accountant, every home in the country needs both. But in the meantime, here's a handful of new barbecue recipes to get you started, and a few useful tips thrown in for free.

'While it's not rocket science, there are a few basic rules to follow to ensure your barbie is a celebration of tender, succulent meat.'

Veal cutlets with warm vegetable salad and salsa verde (see page 102)

VEAL CUTLETS WITH WARM VEGETABLE SALAD AND SALSA VERDE

Serves 4

Yummy; easy; looks good too. Throw a truckload of flat-leaf parsley leaves and a few other bits and pieces in the food processor before you pick up the tongs, and this is 10 minutes' work.

4 veal cutlets
2 zucchini, cut lengthways into 5 mm strips
1 large red capsicum, white insides and
   seeds removed, cut into quarters
1 eggplant, cut lengthways into 1 cm strips
1 head radicchio, quartered through the stem
olive oil, for brushing
sea salt and freshly ground black pepper
⅓ cup olive oil
2 tablespoons white wine vinegar
1 teaspoon Dijon mustard

SALSA VERDE
2 bunches flat-leaf parsley, leaves picked
2 tablespoons lemon juice
3 anchovy fillets
1 tablespoon capers
2 cloves garlic, chopped
½ cup olive oil

To make the salsa verde, place all the ingredients except the oil in a food processor and combine. With the motor running, add the oil gradually until a thick paste forms, then reserve.

Brush the meat and vegetables generously with olive oil, season with salt and pepper, and place on the grill. Once the meat is cooked, transfer it to a large plate, cover loosely with foil and set aside to rest for 5 minutes. Pour any juices from the resting meat over the vegetables as they cook.

Mix the olive oil, white wine vinegar and Dijon mustard in a large bowl and throw in the vegetables as they are cooked, and season well.

Serve a selection of grilled vegetables and a veal cutlet for each person, spooning over the salsa verde.

GRILLED TUNA WITH WARM POTATO SALAD AND FRESH HERBS

Serves 4

This is a nice little something you can throw on the barbie that will double as a flash dinner-party dish. You can make this a team effort by having someone in the kitchen worrying about the potato salad and the herbs, while you worry about cooking the tuna to perfection and enjoying a cold drink.

2 organic or free-range eggs
6 medium-sized kipfler potatoes, peeled
2 spring onions, white and pale green parts only, sliced
½ cup extra virgin olive oil, plus extra for brushing
sea salt and freshly ground black pepper
2 tablespoons lemon juice
1 teaspoon Dijon mustard
1 cup flat-leaf parsley leaves
1 bunch chives, finely chopped
1 bunch chervil, leaves picked
1 bunch oregano, leaves picked
4 × 200–250 g tuna fillets, about 1 cm thick

Place the eggs in a saucepan and cover with cold water. Bring the water to a boil and cook for 4 minutes, then remove from the pan and leave to cool before peeling.

Bring a pan of salted water to a boil and cook the potatoes until just tender. Roughly chop them whilst they are still warm, and crush some with the back of a fork, then transfer to a bowl. Roughly chop the eggs and add to the potatoes along with the spring onions, 2 table-spoons of the oil and plenty of salt and pepper, and set aside.

In a large bowl, combine the rest of the oil with the lemon juice and mustard, season and mix well. Add the fresh herbs and toss to coat them thoroughly, and reserve.

Brush the tuna with some oil, season well, then chargrill for just a few minutes either side until medium–rare.

Place a big spoonful of the potato salad on each plate, add a piece of tuna on top and garnish with the fresh herbs, spooning over any remaining dressing.

Grilled tuna with
warm potato salad
and fresh herbs

MOROCCAN LAMB FILLETS WITH HERB AND CAPSICUM BULGUR

Serves 4

The biggest battle here is figuring out whether these overgrown, couscous-like grains are called bulgur (like burger with an 'l') or burghul (like a house being robbed). Either way, this is a quick and easy barbecue dish that isn't too heavy – perfect for a stinking hot summer's day with a chilled glass of rosé or, even better, sparkling shiraz.

8 metal or bamboo skewers
8 lamb fillets (approximately 60–70 g each)
200 g bulgur
1 red capsicum, white insides and
    seeds removed, cut into 2–3 cm strips
½ yellow capsicum, white insides and
    seeds removed, cut into 2–3 cm strips
2 tablespoons each chopped mint, coriander
    and flat-leaf parsley
2 sun-dried or semi-dried tomatoes, very
    finely chopped
2 tablespoons olive oil
2 tablespoons lemon juice
2 tablespoons pine nuts, toasted
lemon wedges, to garnish

MARINADE
2 cloves garlic, crushed
2 tablespoons olive oil
3 tablespoons lemon juice
1 tablespoon ground coriander
1 tablespoon ground cumin
1 tablespoon ground cinnamon
6 mint leaves, very finely chopped
12 coriander leaves, very finely chopped
sea salt and freshly ground black pepper

To make the marinade, mix the garlic, oil, lemon juice, coriander, cumin, cinnamon, mint and coriander together in a bowl, and season with salt and pepper. Add the lamb and make sure that each fillet is completely coated in the marinade. Cover and refrigerate for 2–4 hours. If using bamboo skewers, soak them in water for 1 hour to prevent them from burning.

Bring the lamb back to room temperature by removing it from the fridge half an hour before cooking.

Meanwhile, pour enough boiling water over the bulgur to cover by 3 cm and set aside for 20 minutes. All the water should be absorbed in this time; drain off any excess liquid. Brush the capsicum with a little oil and chargrill over low heat until tender, then cut crossways into thin slices. In a large bowl, mix the bulgur, grilled capsicum, herbs, tomatoes, olive oil, lemon juice and toasted pine nuts together, and season well.

Thread each lamb fillet onto a skewer, grill for just a minute or two on each side, and serve immediately with the bulgur and a lemon wedge.

BARBECUE MOUSSAKA
Serves 4

Purists will choke on this translation of the classic Greek moussaka for the barbie. Personally, I've always found the original a fairly dull, often stodgy affair, despite my Greek blood. While this isn't really moussaka, the flavours are nice and clean with a satisfying richness from the parmesan béchamel. Posh barbecue fare.

1½ teaspoons dried oregano leaves
1 teaspoon ground cinnamon
1 teaspoon sea salt
2 bay leaves
3 cloves garlic, crushed
⅓ cup olive oil
⅓ cup white wine
8 × 100 g thin lamb leg steaks
4 slices tomato (about 1.5 cm thick)
4 slices eggplant (about 1.5 cm thick)
neutral oil (see page 6), for brushing
sea salt and freshly ground black pepper

BÉCHAMEL SAUCE
100 g butter
150 g plain flour
about 700 ml milk
1 cup grated parmesan cheese
pinch nutmeg
2 tablespoons very finely chopped
   flat-leaf parsley

Mix the oregano, cinnamon, salt, bay leaves, garlic, oil and wine together in a shallow dish and add the lamb steaks, coating them well. Cover and marinate in the fridge for 2–4 hours. Bring the steaks back to room temperature by removing them from the fridge half an hour before cooking.

To make the béchamel, melt the butter in a small pan then gradually add the flour, stirring to make a roux (paste). Cook for a few minutes, stirring constantly, then add the milk gradually, stirring between each addition, until you have a thick sauce. Remove from the heat and stir through the parmesan, nutmeg and parsley, then cover to keep warm.

Chargrill the marinated lamb steaks over high heat. Brush the tomato and eggplant slices with oil and season well with salt and pepper, then chargrill over medium heat.

Place a lamb steak on each plate, top with a slice of eggplant, followed by another lamb steak and finally a slice of tomato. Spoon some béchamel sauce over the top and serve immediately.

CAJUN CHICKEN
SKEWERS AND SALAD
Serves 4

Chicken can be pretty bland on the barbecue, but the addition of plenty of spices can, well, spice it up. While onion, carrot and celery are the basis of many French dishes, the New Orleans equivalent is onion, celery and green capsicum, which is exactly what is in the salad to complement the chook.

1 kg chicken breasts or thigh fillets,
**   cut into 2 cm pieces**
8 metal or bamboo skewers
2 tablespoons olive oil
2 tablespoons lime juice
a few drops Tabasco sauce
sea salt and freshly ground black pepper
1 green capsicum, white insides and
**   seeds removed, cut into 1 cm squares**
2 stalks celery, chopped
1 small red onion, finely sliced
½ large green chilli, very finely sliced
2 tablespoons chopped coriander leaves

CAJUN MARINADE
1 tablespoon celery salt
1 tablespoon paprika
1 tablespoon dried thyme
1 tablespoon dried oregano
½ tablespoon cumin
½ teaspoon cayenne pepper, or more to taste
1 tablespoon neutral oil (see page 6)

Mix all the marinade ingredients together in a large shallow dish. Add the chicken pieces and marinate in the fridge for 2–12 hours.

If using bamboo skewers, soak them in water for 1 hour before use to prevent them from burning. Bring the chicken back to room temperature by removing it from the fridge half an hour before cooking. Thread the chicken pieces onto the skewers and cook on a hot chargrill or flat grillplate until opaque.

Mix the olive oil, lime juice, Tabasco and salt and pepper in a salad bowl. Add the capsicum, celery, onion, chilli and coriander and mix well to coat.

Serve two skewers per person with a generous spoonful of salad.

FRIED SCHOOL PRAWNS

Serves 2

Some things in life you can plan, others are just meant to be. If you happen to spot fresh school prawns at a fish market (most likely between September and Christmas time), you need to buy some and cook them quickly and simply, whether they were on your menu or not.

If the wok-burner on your barbie has some oomph, cook these outside and avoid the fried-prawn smell in the kitchen (to lunatics like me, it's perfume, but my wife and daughter think otherwise).

1 cup plain flour

2 tablespoons table salt (not rock salt)

500 g green (raw) school prawns, shells left on
   (removing the heads is optional)

2 cups neutral oil (see page 6)

1 lemon, cut into quarters, to serve

Homemade Mayonnaise (see page 208), to serve

Mix the flour with the salt in a large bowl and add the prawns, tossing through to coat. Place the prawns in a colander or sieve and gently shake to remove any excess flour.

Heat the oil in a wok or frying pan until very hot, then add half the prawns and cook until crispy and golden brown. Remove and drain on paper towel, then repeat with the second batch of prawns. (If you cook them all at once the prawns will become soggy, as the oil won't be hot enough.)

Serve immediately with some lemon quarters and homemade mayonnaise.

 You can season the flour with a pinch of paprika or cayenne pepper, or plenty of black pepper to give it a kick but, for me, the salty sweetness of the prawns is just perfect.

THYME LAMB BROCHETTES WITH BRAISED SPRING VEGETABLES

Serves 4

The vegetables here are great on their own, but they also work really well with the thyme-scented sweetness of the lamb. Just remember that vegetables in a dish like this have to be really top quality.

You could splurge and use meltingly tender lamb loins if you want.

2 tablespoons olive oil
finely grated zest of ½ lemon
2 cloves garlic, crushed
1 tablespoon fresh thyme leaves
sea salt and freshly ground black pepper
1 x 800 g lean lamb leg or shoulder,
    cut into 2 cm cubes
8 metal or bamboo skewers

BRAISED VEGETABLES
750 g broad beans, shelled
1 clove garlic, finely sliced
1 leek, white part only, sliced
6 tablespoons extra virgin olive oil
1 slice prosciutto, finely sliced
500 g green peas, shelled
½ cup Homemade Chicken Stock
    (see page 208) or water
3 small zucchini, cut into 1 cm pieces
1 bunch asparagus, woody ends discarded,
    cut into 3–4 cm pieces
6 mint leaves, very finely sliced
2 sprigs thyme, leaves picked
1 tablespoon lemon juice

In a shallow dish, combine the olive oil with the lemon zest, garlic, thyme, salt and pepper. Add the lamb, making sure that it is completely coated in the marinade. Cover and refrigerate for 2–12 hours. If using bamboo skewers, soak them in water for 1 hour before use to prevent them from burning. Bring the meat back to room temperature by removing it from the fridge half an hour before cooking.

To double-peel the broad beans, bring some water to a boil in a small saucepan. Add the broad beans and cook them for about 30 seconds, then drain and leave to cool before removing the tough outer skins.

Thread the lamb pieces onto skewers and cook on a hot chargrill until medium–rare.

Meanwhile, in a heavy-based frying pan, soften the garlic and leek in 3 tablespoons of the extra virgin olive oil, then stir through the prosciutto. Add the peas and stock or water and simmer for 5 minutes. Add the zucchini and asparagus and cook for 1 minute more. Add the broad beans and stir just to warm them through, then remove the pan from the heat and add the mint, thyme, lemon juice and the rest of the oil. Transfer to a shallow bowl and serve alongside a platter of the brochettes.

LAMB LOINS IN PROSCIUTTO WITH RADICCHIO AND RED WINE RISOTTO

Serves 4

The flavours in this dish are big and robust, and suit a grown-up palate. The radicchio brings a sharp bitterness, which complements the sweetness of the lamb. This one's ideal for a winter barbie.

1 clove garlic, finely chopped
1 leek, white and pale green parts only, sliced
1 tablespoon olive oil
2 tablespoons butter
1 head radicchio, leaves washed and finely sliced
2 cups arborio, vialone or carnaroli rice
1 cup Homemade Chicken Stock (see page 208)
about 2 cups red wine
3–4 lamb loins of similar thickness (about 200 g each), trimmed of all fat
sea salt and freshly ground black pepper
3–4 thin slices prosciutto
2 tablespoons finely chopped flat-leaf parsley
⅔ cup finely grated parmesan cheese
4 sprigs fresh thyme, leaves picked

In a large, heavy-based pan soften the garlic and leek in the oil and 1 tablespoon of the butter. Add the radicchio leaves and soften them for a minute or so before adding the rice. Stir through so the rice is well coated and cook for a minute more. Add the stock and just enough red wine to cover, then bring to a boil. Simmer for about 17 minutes, gradually adding more wine as it is absorbed by the rice and stirring, until the rice is al dente. Make sure that the final result is wet and soupy, not too firm, by adding a little extra wine or water if necessary.

Meanwhile, season the lamb loins with plenty of pepper and just a little salt. Wrap each loin in a slice of prosciutto and chargrill over high heat until the meat is medium–rare and the prosciutto is nicely crisp (about 7–10 minutes in total). Remove the lamb from the grill and set it aside to rest, loosely covered with foil, for a few minutes.

Remove the risotto from the heat and stir through the parsley, the remaining butter and the cheese, and spoon into four shallow bowls. Slice the lamb and arrange on top of the risotto. Sprinkle thyme leaves over the top and serve.

SKIRT STEAK FAJITAS WITH GUACAMOLE

Serves 4

You could use topside, rump or any other type of beef good for stir-frying in this dish, but skirt makes a nice change and it has plenty of flavour. You can, of course, stir-fry this dish in your wok on the stove, but who needs an excuse to fire up the barbie?

½ teaspoon cayenne pepper
1 teaspoon dried oregano
½ teaspoon ground cumin
½ teaspoon ground allspice
½ teaspoon sea salt
½ teaspoon freshly ground black pepper
2 cloves garlic, crushed
1 tablespoon neutral oil (see page 6)
500 g skirt steak, cut into 5 mm thick slices
plenty of tortillas, to serve

GUACAMOLE
1 avocado, peeled and seed removed, flesh finely diced
½ red onion, finely diced
1 large ripe tomato, seeds removed, flesh finely diced
2 tablespoons chopped coriander leaves
½ medium-sized red chilli, very finely chopped
1 tablespoon olive oil
1 tablespoon lime juice
sea salt and freshly ground black pepper, to taste

Combine the spices, garlic and oil together in a shallow dish. Add the steak, making sure that it is completely coated in the marinade. Cover and refrigerate for 2–4 hours. Bring the steak to room temperature by removing it from the fridge half an hour before cooking.

Make the guacamole by mixing all the ingredients together, and reserve. Turn your oven on to the lowest setting and throw in the tortillas to warm through.

Preheat your flat grillplate to very hot, and cook the marinated steak for about ½–1 minute, turning each piece as it browns. Remove to a serving bowl when just cooked.

Spoon some steak and a dollop of guacamole into a warmed tortilla and serve.

Skirt steak fajitas with guacamole

GRILLED WAGYU WITH EXOTIC MUSHROOMS

Serves 4

Now, there's wagyu and there's wagyu. A grade 1 wagyu steak looks much like a normal piece of meat, with a little marbling through it, while a grade 10 steak is the colour of your hand – it's predominantly fat and incredibly rich, so less is clearly more in this case. And it certainly won't need rich sauces to confuse the issue, which is why this light but intensely flavoured mushroom stir-fry is the perfect partner.

4 × 120 g slices wagyu steak (about 1.5 cm thick)
sea salt and freshly ground black pepper, to taste
5 tablespoons extra virgin olive oil
1 clove garlic, finely sliced
2 spring onions, white and pale green parts only,
    finely sliced diagonally
200 g exotic mushrooms (a mixture of shimeji, enoki,
    wood fungus, shiitake, oyster and pine mushrooms,
    depending on what is in season)
1 tablespoon lime juice
1 tablespoon each finely chopped flat-leaf parsley,
    thyme and oregano

Bring the steaks to room temperature by removing them from the fridge half an hour before cooking. Season them well, then cook on a pre-heated hot flat grillplate for about 3 minutes each side, so that they are medium–rare. Remove from the grill and set aside to rest, loosely covered with foil, for 5 minutes.

Meanwhile, heat 2 tablespoons of the oil in a wok and add the garlic, spring onions and mushrooms, stirring occasionally until the mushrooms start to soften (this will take about a minute), then remove from the heat. Add the rest of the olive oil, the lime juice and herbs and season to taste with sea salt and black pepper. Add any juices from the resting steaks and stir through. Serve each steak topped with a pile of stir-fried mushrooms.

BRUSCHETTA WITH WARM HALOUMI SALAD

Serves 4 as a substantial entrée

Dry-fried haloumi cheese is just fine on its own as far as I'm concerned, but it's also great in a quick salad piled on top of some grilled Italian bread.

For normal people a dish like this is a meal in itself. For more enthusiastic eaters like me, it's a lovely entrée to have before a piece of barbecued meat.

1 large red onion, thinly sliced
⅔ cup extra virgin olive oil
about 16 small black olives
2 tablespoons chopped mint leaves
2 tablespoons chopped flat-leaf parsley
2 sun-dried or semi-dried tomatoes, very finely chopped
3 tablespoons lemon juice
sea salt and freshly ground black pepper
4 thick slices Italian bread
1 clove garlic, cut in half
2 × 250 g packets haloumi cheese, cut into 5 mm slices
4 radicchio leaves, shredded

Cook the onion in 2 tablespoons of the oil over medium heat until golden brown. Set aside and keep warm.

In a bowl, combine the remaining olive oil with the olives, mint, parsley, tomatoes and lemon juice with a little sea salt and plenty of black pepper.

Chargrill the slices of bread, then rub one side with a cut clove of garlic.

Chargrill the haloumi on a very hot flat grillplate until browned on both sides.

Serve a piece of bruschetta topped with radicchio, cheese and onions, then spoon the dressing over and serve immediately.

PROSCIUTTO-WRAPPED SEAFOOD KEBABS WITH TOMATO CHILLI SAUCE

Serves 4

I'm crazy for wrapping all sorts of meat and seafood in a very thin slice of prosciutto before cooking it. The prosciutto adds miles of flavour and crisps up nicely to provide a contrast in texture to the tender meat inside. Here, it also provides protection for the delicate seafood, so it won't go to pieces on your barbie.

8 metal or bamboo skewers
8 medium-sized green (raw) prawns
8 large white scallops, any hard sinew removed
200 g blue-eye, cut into 8 pieces, each 2 cm square
    and 1 cm thick
about 6 thin slices of prosciutto, each cut into
    2.5 cm × 8 cm pieces
16 cherry or grape tomatoes
olive oil, for brushing
freshly ground black pepper

TOMATO CHILLI SAUCE
1 clove garlic, finely chopped
1 red chilli, finely chopped
1 red shallot, finely chopped
1 tablespoon olive oil
1 × 400 g can diced tomatoes
½ teaspoon cumin
½ teaspoon coriander seeds
1 tablespoon chopped fresh coriander leaves
1 tablespoon red-wine vinegar

If using bamboo skewers, soak them in water for 1 hour before use to prevent them from burning.

To make the sauce, soften the garlic, chilli and shallot in oil in a saucepan, then add the remaining ingredients and simmer on low heat for 10 minutes. Set the sauce aside in a warm place while you cook the kebabs.

To prepare the prawns, twist off the head and peel off the shell, removing the dark intestinal tract, and leaving the last section of the tail on.

Wrap each piece of seafood in a strip of prosciutto and thread onto the skewers with the tomatoes (ie start with a piece of blue-eye, followed by a tomato, a scallop, another tomato, a prawn, etc). Brush the kebabs lightly with oil and grill over medium heat until the seafood is just firm to the touch.

Serve two kebabs per person with a grind of black pepper on top, accompanied with the tomato chilli sauce.

The easiest thing to do with seafood on a barbie is overcook it. Wrap an extra piece of fish in prosciutto and use as a 'tester', and remember, the fish will continue to cook once it is removed from the heat.

BEEF AND CAPSICUM KEBABS WITH BARBECUE SAUCE AND 'FRIED' COLESLAW

Serves 4

Just plain silly, but good fun. Here the classic coleslaw ingredients are turned into something resembling a fritter crossed with a hotcake, and the kebabs are spiced up with a yummy barbecue sauce.

8 metal or bamboo skewers

800 g rump steak, trimmed of fat and cut into 2 cm cubes

3 capsicums (1 red, 1 green and 1 yellow), white insides and seeds removed, cut into 2 cm chunks

1 cup plain flour

1 organic or free-range egg, beaten

1 cup very cold beer

¼ small cabbage, very finely sliced

1 small red onion, very finely sliced

1 large carrot, coarsely shredded

½ stalk celery, finely sliced

sea salt and freshly ground black pepper

olive oil, for brushing

about ½ cup neutral oil (see page 6), for frying

BARBECUE SAUCE

2 cups tomato sauce

2 tablespoons brown sugar

½ teaspoon cayenne pepper

2 tablespoons Worcestershire sauce

⅓ cup cider vinegar

2 tablespoons orange juice

½ teaspoon very finely grated orange zest

1 teaspoon mustard powder

If using bamboo skewers, soak them in water for 1 hour before use to prevent them from burning. Alternately thread pieces of steak and capsicum onto the skewers, and reserve.

Combine all the barbecue sauce ingredients in a saucepan, bringing to a boil and simmer for 5 minutes.

In a large bowl, mix the flour, egg and beer together to form a batter. Add the cabbage, onion, carrot and celery to the batter, season and mix well.

Brush the kebabs with olive oil and chargrill, brushing generously with the barbecue sauce for the last couple of minutes of cooking. Once cooked, remove the kebabs from the grill and set aside to rest for a couple of minutes before serving.

Pour the neutral oil on the flat grillplate and, when hot, spoon out four portions of batter mixture (about 2 heaped tablespoons each) to make four fritters. Allow them to brown on one side before turning, then make sure that the batter is cooked through before removing from the barbecue.

Place a couple of kebabs and a coleslaw fritter on each plate, pouring a little extra barbecue sauce over the kebabs.

GARAM MASALA SWORDFISH WITH INDIAN-SPICED VEGETABLES

Serves 4

Let's not pretend that you would find this at your average barbie in Mumbai – the flavours are Indian, but the dish is hardly traditional. But it's just the thing to have while watching the Aussie cricketers play India on the box.

Garam masala is a blend of Indian spices available from supermarkets.

3 tablespoons natural yoghurt

3 teaspoons garam masala

1 teaspoon ground cumin

½ teaspoon ground cinnamon

4 swordfish steaks (or any firm white fish),
   about 1 cm thick

50 g butter

2 tablespoons neutral oil (see page 6),
   plus extra for brushing

1 teaspoon black mustard seeds

1 teaspoon sea salt

1 teaspoon Indian curry powder

8 small new potatoes

2 carrots, cut into 2 cm chunks

12 curry leaves (optional)

12 green beans, cut into 3 cm lengths

6 yellow squash, halved *or* 3 yellow zucchini,
   cut into chunks

lime segments, to garnish

Mix the yoghurt, 2 teaspoons of the garam masala, the cumin and cinnamon together in a shallow dish and add the fish steaks, coating them well. Cover and marinate in the fridge for 2–4 hours. Remove the fish from the fridge half an hour before cooking.

Heat the butter and oil in a wok and add the mustard seeds, salt, the remaining garam masala, the curry powder, potatoes, carrots, and curry leaves, if using, and cook, stirring, for about a minute, until the mustard seeds start to pop. Add ½ cup water and cover tightly with the lid, reducing to a low simmer. Cook for 10–15 minutes, shaking the wok occasionally. Add the beans and squash or zucchini and cook, covered, for 5 minutes more.

Brush some neutral oil on the chargrill and cook the swordfish for about 2 minutes each side until medium–rare. Serve the fish sprinkled generously with sea salt and a squeeze of fresh lime, alongside the spiced vegetables.

 This dish is great cooked on the grill and the wok burner on your barbie, but works just as well cooked inside on the stove, if it's too cold to fire up the beast.

1 THINK ABOUT THICKNESS

If you want your steak medium–rare, the meat must be thick enough to caramelise on the outside while staying pink on the inside; 2–3 cm thick is perfect. If you want your steak well done, a piece about 1 cm thick will do the job. Always buy the best quality meat that you can afford.

2 NO COLD COOKING

Make sure you bring your steak to room temperature before you cook it. This way the inside won't be colder than the outside and the meat will cook evenly.

3 PUT THE OIL ON YOUR STEAKS . . .

. . . not all over the hotplate – that way you won't have the taste of burnt oil through your meat.

7 steps to the perfect steak

4 HOT MEANS HOT

Raw meat will stick like glue to a luke-warm grill. Make sure your grill or frying pan is nice and hot to start with, and you'll get a nice crust on the meat.

5 TURN THE BLOODY STEAKS ONCE!

Not forty times, not even four. Turning only once means the inside stays nice and tender and the outside caramelises to a crust.

6 KEEP IT CLEAN

There are all sorts of nasties in the juices from raw meat, so don't put the cooked meat back to wallow in them – a clean plate is a must.

7 A LITTLE REST ALWAYS HELPS

Rest your cooked steaks for five minutes, loosely covered in foil or a clean tea towel. This allows the juices to settle back into the fibres of the meat, and will ensure a juicy, delicious, perfect piece of steak.

GRANDMA

AUNTY
MAVIS

UNCLE
NORMAN

The host with the most

AUNTY
MAVIS

The host with the most

As you've no doubt worked out by now, we cook differently for our mates than we do for a hot date. And a simple dinner with friends is very different to cooking for your parents' 50th wedding anniversary or your wife's birthday. It's horses for courses.

A great mate of mine once needed an idea for an entrée to go with his only main-course dish: barbecued steak and salad. I recommended the best simple starter I know, figs wrapped in prosciutto with gorgonzola cream sauce. This description is just about the full recipe. Four ingredients. One dish. And it's wonderful. My mate entertained on that for months, showing off his fancy fig dish – he was a one-trick pony, but it was a terrific trick. Then, the panicked phone call came: 'Champ, it's Bruce. There're no more figs, the bloke said they're out of season – what am I going to do?' The answer was not to use dried ones, as he suggested, but instead buy some smoked salmon, lemons and crusty bread and meet asap to discuss further menu development over a beer or two. Not every recipe here is as perfectly simple and simply perfect as Bruce's figs, but you would have to try pretty hard to really mess them up.

Being the host with the most is about knowing when to take it easy and be casual, and when to go that extra yard for a really special occasion. Cooking for a large crowd isn't about showing off your skills rattling a pan or impressing with the most expensive ingredients, it's about putting in the time and effort. Because I'm certifiably mad, I once rustled up a twelve-course sit-down Asian banquet for two dozen, for my mother-in-law's 75th (she made a spectacular entrance flying in on her broom). While you needn't go quite that far, it's handy to have a few tricks up your sleeve for when the hordes descend.

The more people you're feeding, the more you'll need to balance complicated cooked dishes with simpler, probably cold ones. You'll also need plenty of time to plan and get organised – a dinner for a big group doesn't just happen; you need to check you have enough glasses and serving platters, find out if people don't eat meat (they, of course, deserve to have just mashed potato and green salad, but better to be more generous), write your shopping list and stock the booze cupboard.

I hope you'll have a crack at some of the following seasonal, casual, celebration and banquet menus, as there are few things more satisfying than cooking good food for people that you care about.

'A simple dinner with friends is very different to cooking for your parents' 50th wedding anniversary.'

summer menu Serves 4–6

KIMBO'S CHOWDER

This is a fantastic dish with quite a bit of sweetness from the corn, thyme and the seafood itself. It's a beauty for a dinner party because you can cook just about everything ahead of time. Then all you need do is reheat the soup and stir through the seafood and cream just before serving.

1 tablespoon butter
2 thick rashers streaky bacon, rind removed, rashers sliced into thin strips
2 cobs corn
2 carrots, finely diced
2 stalks celery from the inside of the bunch, finely diced
1 leek, white part only, finely diced
1 small brown onion, finely diced
2 desiree or other waxy potatoes, finely diced
1 tablespoon thyme leaves
4 cups Homemade Fish Stock (see page 208)
2 tablespoons brandy
1 tablespoon plain flour, dissolved in ½ cup cold water
250 g white fish fillets (like blue-eye or ling), finely diced
4 large green (raw) prawns or 8 scallops, sliced
½ cup cream
sea salt and freshly ground black pepper

In a large, heavy-based stockpot, melt the butter and add the bacon, lightly browning it.

Stand each corn cob on its end on a chopping board and carefully slice the kernels off with a large knife. Add the corn kernels to the pot, along with the chopped vegetables and the thyme. Stir to coat all the ingredients and cook over a gentle heat for a couple of minutes so that the vegetables are slightly softened but not browned.

Add the fish stock and enough water to completely cover the vegetables. Bring to a boil then simmer over a low heat for 20–30 minutes. Gently stir through the brandy and flour paste and cook for a couple of minutes, then fold through the seafood and cook for 1 minute more. Remove the stockpot from the heat, stir through the cream, season and serve.

PANZANELLA

There's nothing wrong with a simple but delicious Bread and Tomato Salad (see page 16) for beginners or lazy school nights. Panzanella is a slightly posher version of this, but other than some extra slicing and chopping, it is no more difficult.

2 cups day-old sourdough bread, cut into 2 cm cubes
½ cup extra virgin olive oil
¼ cup red-wine vinegar
1 clove garlic, crushed
sea salt and freshly ground black pepper
1 small red onion, finely sliced
2 ripe tomatoes, diced, seeds removed
½ cucumber, peeled, diced and seeds removed
½ green capsicum, white insides and seeds removed, diced
1 tablespoon fresh thyme leaves
10 basil leaves, torn or sliced
½ cup goat's curd or soft goat's cheese

Preheat the oven to 180°C. Spread the cubes of bread out on a baking tray, and bake until they dry out and just start to colour.

In a large salad bowl, mix the oil and vinegar together, then add the garlic and some salt and pepper. Toss through the bread, onion, tomato, cucumber, capsicum and herbs. Check that there is enough dressing to moisten the bread – add more oil and vinegar if needed. Spoon the goat's curd or cheese over the top and serve immediately.

 When you're chopping vegetables, put a tea towel between your chopping board and the kitchen bench to absorb the vibrations and stop the board bouncing back at you.

LAMB RACKS WITH TOMATO AND TAPENADE TARTS

This is the perfect dinner-party main course: a show-off dish that isn't too hard to master. Have a practice run first to get the hang of cooking the puff pastry – it burns easily, but is crook undercooked, so you need to watch it carefully.

1 cup pitted black olives
2 cloves garlic, chopped
6 anchovy fillets
18 basil leaves, 12 kept whole and 6 finely sliced
½ cup olive oil, plus extra for cooking
2 lamb racks (6 or 8 chops on each), trimmed of fat
sea salt and freshly ground black pepper
1 packet frozen puff pastry sheets
4 ripe tomatoes, sliced

Preheat the oven to 200°C. Combine the olives, garlic, anchovies and 12 whole basil leaves using a food processor or a stab blender, gradually adding enough olive oil to make a thick tapenade.

Lightly rub the lamb racks with a little olive oil, season well with salt and pepper and roast for about 15 minutes.

Meanwhile, cut eight circles or squares of puff pastry the same size (about 10 cm across), placing two sheets on top of each other to make four thick tart cases. Transfer to a lightly greased baking tray. Spread about a tablespoon of tapenade on each pastry case, arrange the sliced tomatoes on top and season with salt and pepper. Bake for about 10 minutes, or until the tomatoes are cooked, ensuring that the bases of the pastry cases don't burn.

Rest the meat, loosely covered in foil, for 5 minutes before serving.

Serve each tart topped with basil and sprinkled with sea salt, alongside a lamb rack.

POACHED PEACHES IN BERRY SOUP

This recipe from top chef Serge Dansereau looks spectacular, and has been my traditional celebration of summer berries and stone fruit ever since I first found it back in 1985 in the long-gone *Epicure* magazine. Over the years I've fiddled around with the ingredients, adding the mint and using different kinds of berries to suit the occasion (redcurrants, for example, are only available for about three days in late December, so you have to be on the ball for these).

And while it looks a million dollars, it costs nearly as much – though it is the sort of dessert your guests will remember for a long time.

150 g raspberries
600 ml water
400 g sugar
juice of 1 lemon
6 freestone peaches
50 g blueberries
50 g strawberries, halved or quartered
50 g redcurrants
finely grated zest of ½ grapefruit
1 orange, peeled and pith removed, cut into segments
½ cup finely sliced mint

Purée 100 g of the raspberries until smooth using a stab blender, and set aside.

Bring the water, sugar and lemon juice to a boil in a saucepan and simmer for 10 minutes. Add the whole peaches (ensuring they are completely covered with the syrup), put the lid on and gently poach over low heat for 5–10 minutes, or until the peaches are just tender. Gently remove the peaches from the syrup and peel them as soon as they're cool enough to handle.

Add the puréed raspberries to the syrup and reduce by ⅓ over high heat. Remove the syrup from the heat and add all the remaining berries and the grapefruit zest. When the syrup is completely cool, add the peaches, orange segments and mint and gently stir through before serving.

Overleaf:
Lamb racks with tomato and tapenade tarts
Poached peaches in berry soup

winter menu Serves 4

STRACCIATELLA

This classic Italian soup only works with homemade chicken stock – while you can get away with using ready-made stock in risottos, casseroles and some soups, the stock is definitely the hero in this recipe. It broke my heart the day one of my cooking classes unanimously voted a pleasant-but-daggy chicken pie their favourite dish over what was just about the best version of this I had ever cooked. It was a travesty – trust me, this is simply a great dish.

6 cups Homemade Chicken Stock (see page 208)
sea salt and freshly ground black pepper
½ cup freshly grated parmesan cheese
½ cup finely chopped flat-leaf parsley
1 very fresh large organic or free-range egg,
    lightly beaten

Bring the stock to a boil in a large saucepan and season with salt to taste. Mix the cheese, parsley and egg together in a bowl. When the stock begins to boil, add the egg mixture, stirring vigorously for just a few seconds. Serve immediately, topped with a little freshly ground black pepper.

MARRON WITH VANILLA BUTTER SAUCE

Marron are magnificent-looking, blue-black crustaceans, which you can buy live from serious fish markets, and they give this dish a real wow factor. This classic French sauce also works perfectly well with prawns, bugs, lobster, or a delicate white fish like John Dory. This is an easy dinner-party entrée that will definitely impress, though you'll probably need a practice run with the sauce before attempting it for an audience.

1 cup dry white wine
2 red shallots or ½ small brown onion, chopped
1 vanilla bean, split lengthways
½ cup white-wine vinegar
4 marron, stunned in the freezer for 30 minutes then
    carefully cut in half with a heavy sharp knife
150 g cold butter, chopped into 1 cm chunks
5–6 chives, finely sliced

Preheat the oven to 200°C. Combine the wine, shallot or onion, vanilla bean and white-wine vinegar in a small saucepan, and simmer until reduced to about 2–3 table-spoons of liquid. Strain the sauce through a sieve, discarding the solids, and return the sauce to the pan.
    Bake the marron, cut-side up, for 10 minutes.
    Reheat the sauce until warmed through, then remove from the stove. Stir through the cold butter chunks.
    Arrange the marron on plates and spoon over the sauce. Sprinkle over a few chopped chives and serve.

 Don't split the live shellfish in half in front of the kids – it might upset them. And don't do it in front of the object of your lust either – she might side with the marron.

PORK RACK WITH FENNEL, APPLE AND BALSAMIC VINEGAR

This is one of those terrific, one-pot, bung-it-in-the-oven-and-forget-about-it dishes that works best with really good quality pork. Instead of that awful super-lean stuff, look for free-range or organic pork from specialist producers like Bangalow Sweet Pork, ideally with a good degree of marbling (fat) so the flavour runs right through the meat.

1 pork rack (4–8 ribs), skin removed
   (ask your butcher to do this for you)
2 tablespoons olive oil
sea salt and freshly ground black pepper
2 large bulbs fennel, trimmed, fronds and bulbs
   roughly chopped
8 small new potatoes, cut in half
2 red onions, cut into quarters
100 ml balsamic vinegar
200 ml ready-made veal stock *or* 50–100 ml veal glaze
   diluted with the same amount of water
2 green apples, cored and cut into quarters

Preheat the oven to 200°C. Rub the pork with 1 table-spoon of the oil and season well with salt and pepper. Place the pork in the middle of a large, preferably non-stick, baking dish and scatter the fennel, potatoes and onions all around (or if your baking dish has a rack, place the pork on this and the vegetables in the dish underneath). Sprinkle the vegetables with the rest of the oil and pour over the balsamic vinegar and the stock or glaze. Season with plenty more salt and pepper.

Bake for 1¼ hours, then add the apples to the baking dish. Cook for a further 10 minutes, after which the pork should be just cooked through. Remove the dish from the oven and set aside to rest for at least 10 minutes before carving, to allow all the juices from the resting meat to flavour the vegetables.

Serve the pork ribs on the bone with plenty of vegetables, and some cooking juices spooned over the top. It probably won't be pretty, but it will be bloody delicious.

PECAN, MAPLE SYRUP AND SULTANA BREAD AND BUTTER PUDDING

I feel all wintry just thinking about a sweet baked-custard dessert after some roast pork. Bread and butter puds are just about foolproof; they let you worry about other courses when you want to make a real splash.

⅔ cup sultanas
⅔ cup maple syrup
6 egg yolks from organic or free-range eggs
4 cups milk
⅔ –1 large baguette, cut into 1 cm slices and buttered
1½ cups pecan nuts
½ cup demerara sugar

Soak the sultanas in the maple syrup for 1 hour.

Preheat the oven to 180°C. Beat the egg yolks in a large bowl. Heat the milk in a saucepan until almost boiling, then pour the milk over the egg yolks, whisking quickly so they don't scramble.

Arrange half the bread slices in the bottom of a baking dish, then spread half the pecans on top and pour the sultana and maple syrup mixture over. Arrange another layer of the remaining bread slices and pour the egg mixture carefully over the top.

Sprinkle the remaining pecans and the sugar over the top and bake for about 15 minutes, until the top is browned and the custard is just set.

 It's worth using demerara sugar because the grains don't melt, so they'll stay nice and crunchy.

Overleaf:

Marron with
vanilla butter sauce

Pork rack with fennel,
apple and balsamic vinegar

casual menu Serves 4

ARMANDO'S FIGS AND PROSCIUTTO WITH DOLCE GORGONZOLA CREAM SAUCE

This recipe is adapted from one by Armando Percuoco, from Sydney's Buon Ricordo, and is the best simple dish I know. Armando makes his sauce separately and includes a little butter, but we can make things even simpler. As straightforward as this recipe is, mine still never tastes quite like Armando's.

Keep an eye out for fresh figs for this one.

8 thin slices prosciutto
8 fresh figs
8 toothpicks
about 1 cup cream
1 large tablespoon *dolce* (sweet) gorgonzola cheese

Preheat the oven to 220°C. Wrap a slice of prosciutto around each fig, securing with a toothpick if necessary. Place the figs in a baking dish big enough to fit all the figs without them touching each other. Pour the cream around the figs and crumble over the gorgonzola.

Bake for 5–10 minutes until the prosciutto begins to crisp. Serve two figs per person and spoon over the cream sauce.

PRAWN, FENNEL AND WALNUT SALAD

A very easy dish that is impossible to screw up if you buy good ingredients. It's nice and light, and works well as an entrée before a big meaty main course. There's a satisfying crunch to the walnuts and fennel and an earthy flavour from the walnut oil.

1 cup walnut halves
4 tablespoons good quality walnut oil
2 tablespoons lemon juice
sea salt and freshly ground black pepper, to taste
16–20 fresh, cooked prawns
1 bunch watercress, stalks removed and discarded, tender stems and leaves washed
1 bulb fennel, trimmed and very finely sliced
1 bunch chives, finely chopped

Lightly toast the walnut halves in a hot, dry frying pan, and set aside.

Make the dressing by combining the walnut oil and lemon juice, and season with salt and pepper.

Arrange the rest of the ingredients in a large salad bowl, sprinkling the chives over last. Pour the dressing over the salad and serve.

 Walnut oil is quite strongly flavoured so you may want to mix it with some olive oil. Trust your taste buds – try the dressing first, then tinker with it if you need to.

OSSO BUCO BRAISED IN BALSAMIC VINEGAR

I had a wonderful dish of veal cheeks slow-cooked in balsamic vinegar in San Francisco years ago – the vinegar cut right through the richness of the meat. Veal or beef cheeks are fine to use for this dish, but veal shank is a damn sight easier to find, and just as delicious. Serve this with mashed potato or celeriac and some steamed peas and carrots.

1 bunch thyme
1 stick cinnamon
2 tablespoons olive oil
12 golden shallots, peeled
8 × 3 cm thick pieces veal shank
3 cloves garlic, crushed
120 ml good quality balsamic vinegar
400 ml ready-made veal stock

Preheat the oven to 120°C. Wrap the thyme and the cinnamon stick in muslin and secure with cooking twine.

Heat the oil in a large ovenproof pan with a lid (ideally one that's big enough to accommodate the meat in a single layer), and brown the shallots and the veal pieces on all sides. Add the garlic, balsamic vinegar, stock and the bag of thyme and cinnamon. Bring to the boil, then pop the lid on and transfer the pan to the oven. Bake for 3 hours or until the veal is tender.

 Make this a day or even two days before eating it (if you can make room in your fridge), and it will taste even better.

CHERRIES POACHED IN RED WINE

This is a simple twist on a classic recipe from one of the world's greatest chefs, Joël Robuchon. Recipes from the true greats are normally pretty involved, but you will be surprised at how easy this is (other than pitting the cherries), and it's a great dish for a dinner party without too much fiddling around (other than pitting the cherries).

1 × 750 ml bottle red wine
2 sticks cinnamon
⅔ cup sugar
1 heaped teaspoon cornflour, dissolved in a little water
750 g big ripe cherries, pitted
12 mint leaves, washed and tied in a bunch with cooking twine
thickened cream *or* natural yoghurt, to serve

Pour the wine into a large saucepan and add the cinnamon sticks. Bring to a boil and then turn down to a simmer to reduce the wine by about ⅓. Add the sugar and stir to dissolve, then add the cornflour and water mixture and cook for about 30 seconds.

Add the cherries and bring back to a boil, then pour the mixture into a bowl and add the mint leaves. Cover and chill in the fridge for at least 1 hour. Remove and discard the mint leaves and cinnamon and serve with a dollop of thickened cream or natural yoghurt.

Overleaf:
Armando's figs and prosciutto
with dolce gorgonzola cream sauce
Prawn, fennel and walnut salad

celebration menu Serves 4

ITALIAN SEAFOOD SOUP

There are some great versions of seafood soup, from the bisque to the classic bouillabaisse of southern France. This Italian version is even simpler, and miles away from those horrible 1970s atrocities full of frozen seafood and dried herbs.

The cost of the seafood alone in this dish makes it food for a celebration.

2 tablespoons olive oil
½ stalk celery, sliced
½ bulb fennel, trimmed and sliced
½ brown onion, sliced *or* 1 leek, white and pale green parts only, sliced
1 desiree or other waxy potato, cut into 1 cm cubes
1 clove garlic, finely sliced
½ teaspoon saffron
4 cups Homemade Fish Stock (see page 208)
1 cup tomato passata (puréed tomatoes)
1 cup dry white wine
2 raw blue swimmer crabs, cleaned, each cut into 4 or 6 segments
12 mussels, 'beards' removed, any open shells discarded
200 g blue-eye, bones removed
16 green (raw) prawns, peeled, 8 left whole, 8 cut into four even pieces
2 small fresh squid, cleaned and sliced into rings
1 tablespoon each finely chopped flat-leaf parsley, basil and chives
sea salt and freshly ground black pepper

Heat the oil in a large stockpot and add the celery, fennel, onion or leek, potato, garlic and saffron. Stir well to coat the vegetables in oil, and soften but do not brown. Add the stock, passata and white wine and bring to the boil, then simmer for a couple of minutes before adding the crab – make sure the crab is completely immersed. Simmer for about 5 minutes before adding the mussels, fish, prawns and squid. Simmer for a further minute or two, until the mussels open and the seafood is cooked. Stir through the fresh herbs and season with salt and pepper.

SCALLOPS WITH GARLIC AND PARMESAN

Nothing could be easier than this. The only trick is finding really top quality, very fresh scallops. I like the big, white roe-less Queensland variety for this dish, but whatever you use, make sure that you trim off the little hard sinew on the side of the scallops.

2 cloves garlic, crushed
½–⅔ cup thick cream
½ cup freshly grated parmesan cheese
1 teaspoon very finely chopped flat-leaf parsley *or* ½ teaspoon fresh thyme leaves
12 fresh scallops on the half-shell (preferably the meaty, roe-less type from Queensland), cleaned and trimmed
sea salt and freshly ground black pepper
thin baguette slices, to serve

Mix the garlic, cream, parmesan and parsley or thyme together in a bowl.

Spoon a little of this mixture on top of each scallop, then place them under a hot grill for about 1 minute until they are cooked through. Season and serve with thin baguette slices to mop up the juices.

 The cheese will brown quite quickly, so test a scallop to make sure they are cooked enough. They should be firm, tender and translucent, but not raw.

FAST AND SLOW BEEF

The slow part of this recipe means supervising your slow-cooking beef for about 3 hours, so plan it right and make sure there's a good game of footy to watch on Saturday arvo while it's gently simmering away in the oven.

1.5 kg beef cheeks *or* 1 kg brisket, trimmed and
   cut into 4–5 cm chunks
⅓ cup plain flour
½ cup olive oil, plus 2 tablespoons extra
handful parsley stalks
2 pieces orange peel
2 leeks, white part only, thinly sliced
4 cloves garlic, sliced
1 onion, studded with 6 cloves
1 carrot
½ stalk celery
2 bay leaves
2 cinnamon sticks
1 × 750 ml bottle red wine
½ cup ready-made beef or veal stock diluted with ½ cup water
sea salt and freshly ground black pepper
4 × 3 cm thick slices beef fillet
butter or oil, for frying
2 big handfuls cavolo nero *or* baby spinach,
   washed and trimmed
1 tablespoon balsamic vinegar
fresh thyme leaves, to garnish

Preheat the oven to 150°C. Put the beef chunks in a large plastic bag (check there are no holes) along with the flour and shake to thoroughly coat the meat. Heat ¼ cup of the olive oil in a large ovenproof casserole dish with a lid and brown the meat in batches. Set the browned meat aside and wipe the casserole dish clean.

Wrap the parsley stalks and the orange peel in muslin and secure with cooking twine to make a bouquet garni. Soften the leeks and garlic in the remaining oil in the casserole dish, then add the onion, carrot, celery, bay leaves, cinnamon sticks, bouquet garni and the browned meat. Cover with the wine and stock and season well with salt and pepper. Put the lid on and bring to a boil, then transfer to the oven and cook for 3 hours.

After 2½ hours, remove the beef fillets from the fridge to bring to room temperature. Once cooked, remove the braised beef from the oven and discard the bouquet garni, bay leaves, cinnamon sticks, onion, carrot and celery. Carefully transfer the braised meat to a chopping board and shred with two forks. Return the braised meat to the sauce and reserve.

Season the beef fillets well. Heat a little butter or oil in a frying pan, and cook them over high heat until medium–rare, then set them aside to rest, loosely covered with foil, for 5 minutes. Meanwhile, half-fill a saucepan with salted water and bring to a boil, then add the cavolo nero or spinach and cook until tender. Season with the extra olive oil and balsamic vinegar.

Divide the cavolo nero or spinach among four plates, then spoon a generous amount of braised meat on top, followed by a beef fillet. Spoon over the braising juices and garnish with fresh thyme leaves.

TIRAMISU

You've gotta love this dessert – it holds its own at the swankiest of dinner parties, and is a beauty because you can make it early in the day and it's done and out of the way. Find yourself a bottle of Averna, an Italian digestive, to serve with it, and you're in dessert heaven.

4 organic or free-range eggs, separated
   (you'll need 4 yolks and 3 whites)
125 g icing sugar, sifted
250 g mascarpone cheese
50 ml brandy *or* marsala
400 ml strong black coffee, cooled
200–225 g sponge finger biscuits
50 g dark chocolate, grated
about 2 tablespoons cocoa powder

Lightly beat the egg yolks with the icing sugar until thick and pale then stir through the mascarpone. In a separate bowl, beat the egg whites until soft peaks form, and fold these through the mascarpone mixture.

Mix the brandy or marsala and coffee together in a bowl and dip the sponge biscuits in one by one. In a large rectangular dish that is at least 5 cm deep, arrange a layer of biscuits, followed by a sprinkling of chocolate and a layer of mascarpone mixture. Repeat using the remaining ingredients and finish with a light dusting of sieved cocoa on top. Chill for at least 1 hour before serving.

Overleaf:
Italian seafood soup
Fast and slow beef

Every now and then, an occasion will crop up when you'll have to feed a crowd, be it family, friends or royalty (you never know), and you'll really want to impress. Making a variety of antipasto dishes to serve as appetisers is a great option, as they look spectacular laid out on the table, taste delicious, and can be followed up with a simple main course (such as a one-pot slow-cooked dish or a grill). They can be a lot of work, but if cooking is all about showing generosity of spirit to those you care about, there's no better way to do that than with a table laden with delicious food.

The best antipasto I ever had was at a restaurant in Florence – there were thirty-something plates of food spread over two tables. To my wife's eternal embarrassment, I made four trips to the tables in an attempt to taste every dish (I even managed a couple twice). Following this, we were expected to face pasta, a main course and then dessert. Thinking only of my boyish figure, I skipped dessert.

Here's a selection of antipasto dishes to choose from, some of which can be prepared ahead of time and served cold, cutting down on the amount of work you need to do when your guests arrive. When deciding what to serve, make sure you balance the more complicated dishes with those that don't take as long to prepare (and things that don't even need a recipe, like steamed green beans with oil and red-wine vinegar, top quality olives, or figs cut in half and wrapped in prosciutto). And bear in mind that if you're serving a big, meaty main course, cut down on the meaty appetisers like vitello tonnato – go for lighter seafood or vegetable-based dishes instead.

CAPONATA

1 kg eggplant, cut into 2–3 cm dice
1 cup neutral oil (see page 6)
2 brown onions, sliced
¼ cup olive oil
1 bunch celery, outer stalks removed, pale inner stalks trimmed and sliced
3 ripe tomatoes, peeled and seeds removed, flesh cut lengthways into 1 cm strips *or* 1 x 400 g can diced tomatoes, drained of juice
¼ cup red-wine vinegar
1 tablespoon sugar
1 heaped tablespoon capers
¼ cup roughly chopped large green olives
2 tablespoons finely chopped flat-leaf parsley

Fry the eggplant in batches in the neutral oil until golden brown, then drain on paper towel and reserve.

In a large, deep pan, fry the onions in the olive oil until golden brown, then add the celery and tomatoes and cook until the celery is just soft. Stir through the vinegar and sugar and cook for a few minutes to reduce the vinegar, then add the capers, olives, parsley and eggplant and cook for just 1 minute more.

Leave to cool, and serve at room temperature, or chilled if you prefer.

Antipasto

GOAT'S CURD AND ASPARAGUS FRITTATA

2 teaspoons butter
1 leek, white part only, finely sliced
8 medium-sized asparagus spears, woody ends
    discarded, cut into 1 cm pieces
10 sage leaves, finely sliced
8–10 organic or free-range eggs
150–200 g goat's curd
sea salt and freshly ground black pepper

Melt 1 teaspoon of the butter in a frying pan with a lid
and gently fry the leek, asparagus and sage until the leek
is soft.

Meanwhile, beat the eggs with the goat's curd and
season with salt and pepper, then add the leek mixture
and stir through.

Melt the remaining butter in a non-stick frying pan
and add the egg mixture. Cover loosely with a lid, and
cook over a very low heat without stirring until the egg
has set (about 5 minutes).

When the frittata is cooked, slide it onto a large serving
plate, and serve at room temperature.

PEAS AND BROAD BEANS WITH MINT AND PECORINO

3 cups shelled broad beans
2 cups shelled green peas
⅓ cup extra virgin olive oil
2 tablespoons lemon juice
sea salt and freshly ground black pepper
½ cup grated pecorino cheese
about 8 mint leaves, finely chopped

To double-peel the broad beans, bring some water
to a boil in a saucepan, then add the broad beans and
cook for 30 seconds. Drain and leave to cool for a few
minutes, then remove the tough outer skins.

Cook the peas in plenty of boiling water until tender,
then drain and plunge into iced water for 5 minutes.
Drain once more and combine with the broad beans in
a shallow bowl.

Add the oil and lemon juice and season with salt
and pepper. Top with the pecorino and mint and serve
immediately.

PICKLED FENNEL AND CURED MEATS

1 cup white-wine vinegar
4 cloves
1 large bulb fennel,
  trimmed and finely sliced
freshly ground black pepper
about 2 dozen slices of various cured meats

Pour 2 cups of water into a large saucepan with the
vinegar and cloves and bring to a boil. Add the fennel,
remove the pan from the heat straightaway and leave
to cool, then cover and place in the fridge for 4 hours.

   To serve, remove the cloves and drain the liquid away.
Serve the fennel seasoned with black pepper alongside
a selection of cured meats.

SEAFOOD SALAD WITH LEMON VINAIGRETTE

⅓ cup extra virgin olive oil
2 tablespoons lemon juice
2 tablespoons finely chopped flat-leaf parsley or dill
1 clove garlic, very finely diced
1 small red chilli, very finely diced (optional)
sea salt and freshly ground black pepper
12 medium-sized green (raw) prawns
⅓ cup dry white wine
12 small black mussels, 'beards' removed,
  any open shells discarded
18 pippies or clams
2 medium-sized or 4 small fresh squid, cleaned
  and sliced into rings, retaining tentacles

In a large salad bowl, mix together the oil, lemon juice,
parsley or dill, garlic and chilli, if using, and season.

   To prepare the prawns, twist off the head and peel off
the shell, leaving the last section of the tail on. Remove
the dark intestinal tract.

   In a large stockpot with a lid, bring the white wine to
a boil. Add the mussels, place the lid back on the pot and
cook for 1 minute, then add the pippies or clams and cook
until the shells have opened. Remove with a slotted
spoon and break off the empty half of the shell from each
shellfish and discard. Place the shells with the meat
attached in the dressing.

   Put the prawns and squid into the wine mixture, which
will be enriched with the juices from the shellfish. Bring to
the boil again, place the lid on, then remove from the heat
(the prawns and squid should cook in the time it takes the
liquid to boil). Transfer the seafood to the salad bowl,
along with a couple of tablespoons of the strained cooking
liquid, and serve.

SWEET-AND-SOUR FISH, VENETIAN-STYLE

sea salt and freshly ground black pepper
12 fillets garfish, sand whiting or other small,
    firm white fish
1 tablespoon olive oil
2 tablespoons extra virgin olive oil, plus ½ cup extra
2 brown onions, sliced
¼ cup pine nuts, toasted
2 tablespoons sultanas, soaked in a little white wine
2 tablespoons chopped flat-leaf parsley
½ cup white-wine vinegar

Season the fish fillets with salt and pepper, then fry them in a non-stick pan in the olive oil. Arrange the cooked fish on a serving plate in one layer.

Add 2 tablespoons of extra virgin olive oil to the pan and gently cook the onions until soft and golden (don't let them turn brown). Transfer the onions to a bowl, leave to cool slightly, then mix through the pine nuts, sultanas, parsley, vinegar and the extra oil. Spoon this over the fish and serve.

VITELLO TONNATO

2 whole veal fillets
¼ cup olive oil
sea salt and freshly ground black pepper
200 g good quality canned tuna in oil
1½ tablespoons capers, roughly chopped,
    plus extra to garnish
6–8 anchovy fillets
1½–2 cups Homemade Mayonnaise (see page 208)
pinch white pepper
1 tablespoon lemon juice

Preheat the oven to 200°C. Coat the veal fillets in a little olive oil and season with salt and pepper. Bake for about 15 minutes or until pink, then remove from the oven and leave to cool.

Make the dressing by placing all the remaining ingredients in a food processor and mixing until smooth. Add a teaspoon or two of water if the sauce is too thick.

Thinly slice the veal fillets, arrange the slices in a single layer on a platter and cover with the sauce. Top with extra capers and serve.

If someone had told me when I started my cooking school that the Asian food classes would be the most popular, I would have said they were barking mad. But it seems that we Aussies are in love with the big, clean flavours of Asian food, and while we've been eating at Asian restaurants for years, we increasingly want to learn how to make authentic Asian dishes at home. While Gen Y-ers may prefer the spicier Asian flavours they grew up with, I'm still a sucker for Cantonese food, especially on days when I've got a hangover (which is most days with a 'y' in them). Nowadays, modern Asian food is becoming more popular – traditional Asian food (Japanese, Chinese, Thai, Malaysian and Vietnamese, plus other regional cuisines) prepared with quality local ingredients, often using a blend of Eastern and Western cooking techniques.

The following recipes form a banquet for a special occasion, and borrow from many styles of Asian cooking. They include some of my all-time favourite Asian dishes. Don't be intimidated by the recipe names – they are all easy to master with a bit of practise. For example, you don't need to be a Guangzhou native to cook a good master stock – it's actually really simple, and it's the basis for many tasty Asian dishes.

Before you start cooking, you'll need to take a trip to an Asian food store to stock up on exotic goodies such as cassia bark, star anise, fish sauce and kecap manis. These ingredients are mostly pretty cheap, and the shopping trip is half the fun. So make your list, head for your nearest decent Asian market, roll up your sleeves and you'll create an Asian feast as quick as you can say galangal.

Asian Banquet

KIMBO'S MURTABAKS

1 tablespoon neutral oil (see page 6)
250 g brown onions, very finely diced
½ teaspoon turmeric
½ teaspoon sea salt
250 g beef mince
2 teaspoons oyster sauce
1 teaspoon ground coriander seeds
1 teaspoon ground star anise
12 cardamom seeds, ground
1 packet chilled (not frozen) filo pastry
sweet chilli sauce, to serve

Heat the oil in a wok or large frying pan and soften the onions, then add the turmeric, salt and mince and fry until the meat is cooked through but not browned. Stir through the oyster sauce and the spices, then remove from the heat and leave to cool.

Preheat the oven to 200°C and line a flat baking tray with baking paper. Working with one sheet of pastry at a time (and keeping the rest covered with a damp tea towel so they don't dry out), cut out rectangles of approximately 10 cm x 16 cm, then place about 2 teaspoons of the filling in the centre of one of the long ends of the pastry. Fold over once, then tuck in the ends and roll up. Repeat this process with the remaining mixture, then transfer the rolls to the baking tray and cook for 10–15 minutes, or until the pastry is crisp and golden brown. Serve with sweet chilli sauce alongside.

CRABMEAT WITH SOFT EGGS

1 tablespoon neutral oil (see page 6)
6 organic or free-range eggs, beaten
1 teaspoon light soy sauce
½ teaspoon sea salt
½ teaspoon sesame oil
1 cup cooked crab meat (make sure you remove any remaining bits of shell or cartilage)
2 spring onions, dark green part only, thinly sliced
steamed rice, to serve

Heat the oil in a wok or large frying pan over low heat. Combine all the remaining ingredients and add to the wok. Cook, stirring gently, until the eggs are just beginning to set. Serve with steamed rice.

CHINESE DUCK AND VEGETABLE CRÊPES

4 fresh or dried shiitake mushrooms
1 packet Peking duck pancakes
1 teaspoon neutral oil (see page 6)
1 x 2 cm piece ginger, peeled and grated
½ clove garlic, minced
2 spring onions, finely sliced
2 cups bean sprouts
½ Asian-style roast duck, meat and skin removed
   from bones and thinly sliced
1 teaspoon oyster sauce
1 tablespoon hoisin sauce

If using dried mushrooms, soak them whole in hot water for 10 minutes then drain. Finely slice the mushrooms.

Steam the pancakes in a bamboo steamer until warm, or cheat by warming them in the microwave for a few seconds.

Heat a wok or large frying pan until very hot, then add the oil, ginger, garlic, spring onion and sliced mushroom and cook for 1 minute, stirring constantly.

Add the bean sprouts and cook for another minute, stirring occasionally. Fold through the duck and the sauces and cook for 1 minute more, then transfer the mixture to a bowl.

Place a tablespoon of the mixture into each steamed pancake, roll up and serve.

MASTER STOCK SALMON AND BLUE-EYE

250 g salmon or ocean trout fillets,
   skin on, pin bones removed, cut into 4 cm cubes
250 g blue-eye or other firm white fish, skin on,
   cut into 4 cm cubes
8 spring onions, cut into 8–10 cm lengths
steamed rice, to serve

MASTER STOCK
4 star anise
100 g yellow rock sugar
100 ml light soy sauce
200 ml mirin or Chinese rice wine
1 piece dried orange or tangerine peel, about 2 cm x 4 cm
1 stick cassia bark
1 knob ginger (about 3 cm long), peeled and sliced
1 clove garlic, peeled
   and sliced

To make the stock, place all the ingredients into a stockpot and add a litre of cold water. Bring to a boil and cook for a couple of minutes until the sugar has dissolved. Reduce the heat and simmer, uncovered, for 15 minutes.

Add the fish and spring onions into the simmering stock, place the lid on the pot immediately and, turning off the heat, allow the fish to steep for about 20 minutes. Transfer the fish and spring onions to a shallow bowl, spoon over some of the master stock, and serve with steamed rice.

Master stock can re-used – just make sure you re-boil it for a few minutes beforehand.

PORK RIBS WITH CARAMEL SAUCE

4 cups Master Stock (see opposite recipe)
1 kg American-style pork spare ribs, cut in half
    lengthways (ask your butcher to do this for you)
neutral oil (see page 6), for frying

CARAMEL SAUCE
½ cup grated palm sugar
1 tablespoon grated ginger
2 tablespoons lime juice
1 tablespoon fish sauce
1 large red chilli, seeds removed,
    finely sliced (optional)

Bring the master stock to a boil in a large stockpot.
Add the ribs to the pot, turn the heat down and gently
simmer for 1 hour. Carefully remove the ribs, drain on
paper towel and leave to cool, then cut into individual ribs.

Meanwhile, to make the sauce, dissolve the palm
sugar in ¼ cup of water in a small saucepan. Cook until
the sugar has caramelised to a golden colour, then
remove from the heat and stir through the ginger, lime
juice, fish sauce and chilli (if using).

Pour oil into a shallow pan to a depth of about 1 cm.
Heat the oil to a high temperature (test by throwing in
a cube of bread – if it sizzles, the oil is hot enough). Fry
the ribs in batches until crisp and golden brown, then
drain on paper towel. Serve the ribs piled on a plate with
the hot sauce spooned over.

INDONESIAN BRAISED CHICKEN

2 tablespoons neutral oil (see page 6)
4 chicken thigh fillets, trimmed of fat and
    cut into quarters
2 sticks lemongrass, split lengthways
2 sticks cassia bark
1 teaspoon nutmeg, preferably freshly grated
1 teaspoon whole cloves
⅓ cup kecap manis
1 tablespoon light soy sauce
1 teaspoon sugar
1 tablespoon strained tamarind pulp
steamed rice, to serve

PASTE
3 cloves garlic, roughly chopped
2 medium-sized red chillies, roughly chopped
3 red shallots, roughly chopped
1 knob ginger (about 3 cm long), roughly chopped
1 knob galangal (about 3 cm long), roughly chopped
3 coriander roots, washed and roughly chopped
1 teaspoon peanut oil
1 teaspoon sea salt

Pound all the paste ingredients together in a mortar and pestle or mix in a food processor until a thick paste forms.

Heat the oil in a large wok over very high heat and brown the chicken pieces in batches, then reserve.

Add the paste to the wok and cook for a few minutes over high heat. Return the chicken to the wok, add all the other ingredients and reduce to a simmer. Cook for 10 minutes, adding a little water if the mixture starts to look dry. Serve with steamed rice.

TURMERIC CURRY OF JOHN DORY

1 tablespoon neutral oil (see page 6)
1 cup coconut milk
2 tablespoons grated palm sugar
3 tablespoons fish sauce
1 cup coconut cream
600–800 g John Dory fillets, sliced into 2 cm wide pieces
100 ml fresh lime juice
½ cup coriander leaves, to garnish
steamed rice, to serve

CURRY PASTE
2 dried red chillies, softened in
    very hot water for a few minutes
1 fresh red chilli
½ teaspoon sea salt
2 teaspoons turmeric
1 stick lemongrass, sliced
2 cloves garlic, roughly chopped
4 coriander roots, washed and roughly chopped
2 red shallots, peeled and sliced
4 kaffir lime leaves, very finely sliced
fresh coriander leaves, to garnish

Pound all the curry paste ingredients together in a mortar and pestle, or mix in a food processor, to form a thick paste.

In a shallow heavy-based pan, heat the oil and fry the curry paste for 1 minute. Add the coconut milk, palm sugar, fish sauce and coconut cream and simmer for a few minutes, making sure that the sugar is completely dissolved. Add the fish pieces and gently simmer until the fish becomes opaque (5–10 minutes – be careful not to overcook them), then immediately remove from the heat and stir through the lime juice. Transfer to a serving dish, top with fresh coriander and serve with steamed rice.

School-night staples

School-night staples

You don't need kids to appreciate that Mondays to Thursdays are school nights, and therefore not conducive to too much creative thinking and effort in the kitchen (or anywhere else, for that matter). We get home from a tough day at work, change into glamorous trackies or shorts and T-shirts, and pour ourselves a drink or six. This is not the time to be contemplating hours of cooking.

For some, school-night cooking means microwaving some two-minute noodles or a 21st-century TV dinner, but I've always loved my tucker too much to even consider that sort of rubbish. And there are plenty of simple meals you can cook that you don't even need recipes for – grilled steak or lamb cutlets with vegetables or salad, cold meats or seafood and a salad in summer or bangers and mash in winter – but the boredom threshold can be pretty low if you're eating these day in, day out. What you really need is a collection of tasty and interesting dishes that you can whip up in 20 minutes with no trouble at all.

At Chez Terakes, it's all about using the ingredients that are already in the pantry or that we can quickly grab on the way home to create dishes with the minimum of fuss (and that our eight-year-old daughter Zoe will eat). We tend to have lots of risottos, stir-fries and pasta dishes, and mussels are delicious and really quick to cook. And then there's the ultimate comfort food, the classic roast chook, which is guaranteed to put a smile on your face, even after the worst day at the office (especially when served with my deluxe creamy mash).

Of course, there will always be nights when exhaustion is the winner, and takeaway is the only way. But if you enjoy your food, it's great to have a bunch of favourite recipes at hand that are more interesting than a grill and vegetables, but really no more effort.

'What you really need is a collection of tasty and interesting dishes that you can whip up in 20 minutes with no trouble at all.'

Italian sausage and
vegetable soup (see page 160)

ITALIAN SAUSAGE AND VEGETABLE SOUP

Serves 2

This is a meal, not an entrée, because boy, it's filling. The joy of it is that the vegetables, the pasta and the sausages can all cook at the same time and come together in a soupy, stewy finale.

2 tablespoons olive oil
1 leek, white and pale green parts only, sliced
2 desiree or other waxy potatoes, cut into 1 cm dice
1 carrot, sliced
1 stalk celery, sliced
1 clove garlic, finely chopped
4 cups Homemade Chicken Stock (see page 208)
2–3 tablespoons dried small pasta shells (optional)
3 good quality Italian sausages
1 tablespoon chopped flat-leaf parsley
2 tablespoons freshly grated parmesan cheese

Heat the oil in a large, heavy-based saucepan and gently soften the vegetables and garlic over low heat, without browning them.

Add the chicken stock and pasta, if using, and simmer until the vegetables are cooked but not mushy (15–20 minutes). The soup should be very thick.

Meanwhile, grill or dry-fry the sausages until just cooked through, then slice and add to the soup, simmering for just a minute or two. Serve topped with some parsley and grated parmesan.

ICEBERG LETTUCE WITH BLUE CHEESE AND BACON DRESSING

Serves 2

Too, too easy, and a yummy change from your average green salad. This works nicely as an entrée or to partner a grilled steak.

1 rasher bacon
¾ cup Homemade Mayonnaise (see page 208)
   or good quality ready-made mayonnaise
½ cup blue cheese
1 tablespoon buttermilk
1 tablespoon lemon juice
½ teaspoon Tabasco sauce
freshly ground black pepper
½ iceberg lettuce, washed, drained and
   cut in half

Grill or fry the bacon until crispy, leave to cool slightly then crumble into small pieces.

Mash the mayonnaise, blue cheese, buttermilk, lemon juice, Tabasco and pepper together with a fork until smooth. Pour the dressing over the lettuce wedges and top with the crumbled bacon.

 Make double the dressing – it will keep for days in the fridge in a tightly sealed container.

Iceberg lettuce with blue cheese
and bacon dressing

LAMB LOIN WITH PEA AND BASIL SAUCE

Serves 2

This is the most versatile sauce I know, and one of the yummiest. It works a treat with lamb, but also goes well with chicken breasts, veal fillets, white fish fillets and even scallops. It's a great sauce to master because it gives you so many options.

1 or 2 lamb loins (about 200 g each), trimmed of all fat
1 tablespoon olive oil
sea salt and freshly ground black pepper
25 g butter
1 leek, white and pale green parts only,
    roughly chopped
1 cup shelled green peas
about 20 basil leaves
½ teaspoon sea salt
½ cup Homemade Chicken Stock (see page 208) or water
100 ml cream
roast or boiled potatoes, to serve

Preheat the oven to 200°C. Rub the lamb loins with olive oil, place in a large baking dish and season well. Roast for 15 minutes, then remove from the oven and set aside to rest, loosely covered with foil, for 5 minutes.

Meanwhile, to make the sauce, melt the butter in a saucepan and add the leek, softening it but being careful not to brown it. Add the peas, basil, salt and stock or water, and simmer for between 5–10 minutes, until the peas are just cooked. Remove from the heat and purée with a stab blender, then return the pan to the heat and stir through the cream (do not allow the sauce to boil).

Slice the lamb and serve on a bed of sauce with some roast or boiled potatoes.

 You don't need a green veg with this, the sauce does the trick.

SPRING SALAD WITH ROASTED BEETROOT

Serves 2

This is more a set of guidelines than a recipe. There is everything in this salad bar the kitchen sink, but you can use whatever you have at hand, as long as it's really fresh and green and crisp. Roast the beetroot in advance (you could whack it in the oven before the Sunday-night movie starts), so you can whip this up in no time on a school night.

½ bunch medium-sized fresh beetroot,
    tops trimmed
butter, for cooking
sea salt and freshly ground black pepper
about 10 sage leaves
olive oil, for frying
4 baby zucchini with flowers attached
½ cup shelled broad beans
1 bunch asparagus, cut into 3 cm lengths
1 cup broccoli florets
1 cup sugar snap peas
3 tablespoons walnut oil
2 tablespoons white wine vinegar
½ cup goat's curd
¼ cup pine nuts or walnuts, toasted

Preheat the oven to 200°C.

Wrap each beetroot, along with ½ teaspoon butter and some salt and pepper, in foil, and roast on a baking tray for about 30 minutes, or until tender. Remove from the oven, take off the foil and set the beetroot aside until cool enough to handle. Remove the remaining stalks and rub the skins off with your fingers, then cut each beetroot into quarters.

Fry the sage leaves in a little olive oil until crisp, then drain on paper towel. Reduce the heat a little and fry the whole zucchini on all sides for a minute or two until softened.

To double-peel the broad beans, bring some water to a boil in a saucepan, then add the broad beans and cook for 30 seconds. Drain and leave to cool for a few minutes, then remove the tough outer skins.

Steam the asparagus, broccoli and sugar snaps until tender, then set aside to cool. In a large salad bowl, make a dressing by mixing the walnut oil and vinegar with some salt and pepper. Add the zucchini flowers, asparagus, broccoli, sugar snaps and broad beans and toss through to coat in the dressing. Gently fold in the beetroot, then spoon over the goat's curd and add the sage and toasted nuts, and serve.

STIR-FRIED CHICKEN WITH THAI BASIL AND EXOTIC MUSHROOMS
Serves 2

The dark, rich flavours of the oyster and fish sauces and the aromatic kaffir lime produce a distinctive, delicious dish – you'd hardly know it takes all of 10 minutes to cook. The exotic mushrooms (now not nearly as exotic because they're available almost everywhere) make this a very flash school-night dish.

2 tablespoons neutral oil (see page 6)
300 g boneless chicken thighs, skin removed,
    cut into 2 cm chunks
1 small knob ginger (about 3 cm),
    peeled and cut into very fine strips
2 cloves garlic, finely sliced
4 kaffir lime leaves, finely shredded
250 g selection of exotic mushrooms
    (like shimeji, black fungus and oyster)
1 red chilli, seeds removed, finely sliced (optional)
½ teaspoon sugar
1 tablespoon oyster sauce
1 tablespoon fish sauce
about 20 Thai basil leaves
steamed rice, to serve

Heat the oil in a wok, then add the chicken, ginger, garlic and lime leaves and stir-fry until the chicken is almost cooked. Add the mushrooms, chilli (if using), sugar, oyster and fish sauces. Stir to combine all the ingredients and add the basil leaves just before serving. Serve with steamed rice.

HINGARA'S PORK CHOPS IN BBQ SAUCE
Serves 2

I ate at a humble little restaurant in Sydney's Chinatown called Hingara just about every week for 29 years, until it changed hands in 2000. It saw me through many first dates as a callow youth, hundreds of family dinners, and at least a thousand hangovers as a callow adult.

All that you need for this slightly spicy dish are some sauces and rice wine from an Asian supermarket, and some thin-cut pork chops from an Asian butcher.

250 g pork chops (ideally from an Asian
    butcher), sliced about 1 cm thick,
    cut into 2–3 cm pieces
about 1 cup neutral oil (see page 6)
3 spring onions, white and pale green parts only,
    cut into 2–3 cm lengths
1 tablespoon chilli bean sauce
2 tablespoons Chinese BBQ sauce
4 tablespoons plum sauce
steamed rice and steamed Asian greens,
    such as choy sum or bok choy, to serve

MARINADE
½ teaspoon sea salt
½ teaspoon sugar
½ teaspoon five-spice powder
pinch bicarbonate of soda
2 tablespoons Chinese rice wine

Mix the salt, sugar, five-spice powder, bicarbonate of soda and rice wine together in a shallow dish, and add the pork chops, coating them well. Cover and marinate in the fridge for 2–4 hours or overnight. Bring the pork to room temperature by removing it from the fridge half an hour before cooking.

Pour the neutral oil into a wok or large frying pan to a depth of 2 cm. When the oil is really hot, deep-fry the pork in batches until golden brown, then set aside on a plate lined with paper towel. Drain off all but 1 tablespoon of the oil, and fry the spring onions in this for about ½ minute. Return the pork to the pan, along with the three sauces. Stir-fry for 1 minute, then serve immediately with steamed rice and Asian greens.

Hingara's pork chops
in BBQ sauce

HOKKIEN NOODLES WITH CHINESE ROAST PORK AND PRAWNS

Serves 2

A noodle stir-fry can be a well-planned affair, or just something you throw together with whatever you have at hand: chicken, pork, prawns or Chinese sausage, and any sort of Asian vegetables. I like hokkien noodles because they don't need soaking or pre-cooking; they just go straight in the wok. You'll find that their volume is deceptive – one packet makes a truckload.

You can get the noodles, Chinese roast pork and lup cheong from Asian supermarkets.

1 tablespoon neutral oil (see page 6)
8 green (raw) prawns (frozen prawns are
    OK for this, just thaw before use)
1 lup cheong (Chinese dried sausage), finely sliced
1 cup thinly sliced Chinese roast pork
1 spring onion, white and pale green parts only,
    cut into 2 cm lengths
1 clove garlic, finely sliced
½ knob ginger (about 3 cm long), thinly sliced
2 choy sum, washed and cut into individual leaves
1 medium-sized red chilli, seeds removed,
    finely sliced (optional)
½ small packet fresh hokkien noodles
1 tablespoon oyster sauce
2 teaspoons fish sauce

Heat a wok until hot then add the oil, followed by the prawns, lup cheong, Chinese roast pork, spring onions, garlic and ginger and cook on high heat, stirring occasionally. When the prawns begin to change colour, add the choy sum, chilli (if using) and the noodles. Cook for a minute or so, just to heat the noodles through, then stir through the sauces and serve.

PENNE WITH PRAWNS, BASIL, ASPARAGUS AND TOMATOES

Serves 2

This has been a favourite school-night dish at my place for the best part of ten years. It's a clean, simple dish that's so easy to throw together. Just stop at a fishmonger and a good greengrocer on your way home.

12 medium–large green (raw) prawns
200 g dried penne
4 thick asparagus spears, woody ends discarded,
    cut into 1 cm lengths
50 ml olive oil
1 small leek, white part only, thinly sliced
2 cloves garlic, thinly sliced
½ punnet ripe cherry tomatoes
50 ml good quality extra virgin olive oil
12 basil leaves, torn
sea salt and freshly ground black pepper

To prepare the prawns, twist off the head and peel off the shell, removing the dark intestinal tract, and leaving the last section of the tail on.

Bring a large saucepan of salted water to a boil, slide in the pasta and cook until al dente. Just before you take the pasta off the heat, add the asparagus pieces to the boiling water and cook for about 30 seconds.

Meanwhile, heat the 50 ml of olive oil in a large frying pan and cook the leek, garlic and prawns, without browning the vegetables. When the prawns are cooked, add the tomatoes and cook for a minute or so.

Drain the cooked pasta and asparagus well and add to the prawn mixture. Stir through the extra virgin olive oil and basil, season well, and serve.

Penne with prawns, basil, asparagus and tomatoes

RATATOUILLE MUSSELS

Serves 2

Here, you are essentially taking the ingredients for a classic ratatouille, chopping them into smaller pieces so they cook more quickly, and adding some mussels. This makes an entrée for 3–4 or a light school-night dinner for 2.

2 tablespoons olive oil
½ red onion, finely diced
1 clove garlic, finely diced
½ small eggplant *or* 1 miniature/finger eggplant, finely diced
1 small red capsicum, white insides and seeds removed, finely diced
1 zucchini, finely diced
1 kg small black mussels, 'beards' removed, any open shells discarded
1 cup tomato passata (puréed tomatoes)
½ cup chopped basil leaves
½ cup chopped flat-leaf parsley
freshly ground black pepper

In a large stockpot with a lid, heat the oil then add the onion, garlic, eggplant, capsicum and zucchini and cook until slightly softened but not browned.

Add the mussels and tomato passata and place the lid on the pot. Cook for a few minutes until all the mussels have opened, then add the herbs and black pepper, stir through and serve.

ROAST CHOOK AND MASHED POTATOES

Serves 4

Here are the two golden rules for a good roast chook: start with an absolutely top quality chicken, and don't smother the flavour – though if you're using a cardboard-flavoured frozen number, roll out the spices! You should really truss the thing with string (but then you should also say your prayers at night, and not yell at dickheads in the traffic – so maybe just add it to your To Do list and forget about it).

For the mash, I've always had two sorts in my repertoire – the sensible one with milk and a bit of butter, and the deluxe version with truckloads of butter, a pile of salt and some cream. It depends on what kind of day you've had as to which one you choose.

1 large, preferably organic, chicken
sea salt and freshly ground black pepper
2 tablespoons softened butter
1 lemon
2 tablespoons plain flour
1 cup Homemade Chicken Stock (see page 208)
steamed greens, to serve

DELUXE MASH

600 g desiree or other waxy potatoes,
   peeled and quartered
1 tablespoon sea salt, plus 1 heaped teaspoon extra
100 g butter
2 tablespoons cream

Preheat the oven to 190°C. Pat the chicken dry with paper towel and remove the neck and any excess fat from the cavity. Season inside and out with salt and pepper, then rub the softened butter all over the outside of the chook to help it brown. Push the lemon inside the cavity of the chicken, and transfer the chook to a non-stick baking dish.

Roast for 50 minutes (to test if it's cooked, stick a skewer into the thickest part of the thigh – if the juices are clear, not bloody, it's done).

Meanwhile, boil the spuds in enough water to cover them, with 1 tablespoon of salt added, until cooked.

Remove the chicken from the oven and rest, loosely covered with foil, for 5 minutes, before transferring to a chopping board, draining all the juices back into the baking dish. Pour off any excess fat from the baking dish and gently heat the remaining juices. Add the flour and stir well, scraping up any chicken-y bits off the bottom of the pan. Add the stock and bring to the boil for a few minutes, adding water if needed to get to a gravy-like consistency.

Drain the spuds and return them to the pan. Add the butter, cream and 1 heaped teaspoon of sea salt and mash until creamy.

Carve the chook and serve with plenty of mash and gravy, and steamed greens.

 Drying the chook well with paper towel will help it to crisp up rather than steam in the oven.

LARB

Serves 2

A bit of chopping, a quick trick toasting some rice and pounding it up, and this is the easiest, most delicious Asian dish that you can make. The meat is cooked in water, not oil, and flavoured with a truckload of fresh herbs, chilli, lime juice and fish sauce to give it the classic Thai balance of hot, sweet, salty and sour flavours.

1 tablespoon long-grain or jasmine rice
¼ teaspoon sea salt
½ teaspoon sugar
400 g lean minced chicken or pork
⅓ cup Homemade Chicken Stock (see page 208) or water
4 red shallots, peeled and finely sliced
2 sticks lemongrass, trimmed and very finely sliced
2 red chillies, seeds removed, finely sliced
½ cup fresh lime juice, or more to taste
2 tablespoons fish sauce
2 tablespoons finely chopped mint
2 tablespoons finely chopped coriander
lettuce cups or steamed rice, to serve

To make the toasted rice, simply dry-fry the rice until it starts to turn a pale golden-brown colour. Transfer to a mortar and pestle or a food processor and grind to a fine powder.

In a bowl, stir the salt and sugar through the minced meat. Heat the stock or water in a wok and, as it starts to boil, add the mince, stirring until just cooked (about 2 or 3 minutes).

Place the meat in a bowl and add all the remaining ingredients except the mint and coriander. When the meat has cooled to room temperature, stir through the fresh herbs. Taste, and add more lime, chilli, fish sauce or even a teaspoon of caster sugar if you think the dish needs it. Serve in lettuce cups like san choy bau, or simply with steamed rice.

 Don't rub your eyes or the wedding tackle after chopping chillies. You can't say you weren't warned.

TUNA SASHIMI AND MESCLUN SALAD WITH PONZU DRESSING

Serves 2

If you feel like something light on a summer's night, this is the go. Truth is, this is girl food, so make it on a day when you've already murdered a 700 g steak for lunch. You'll find the citrussy ponzu sauce makes for an interesting dressing.

150 g sashimi-grade tuna, finely sliced
10 g dried wakame (seaweed), softened
   in water and drained (optional)
100 g mesclun salad mix
½ small cucumber, skin and seeds removed,
   cut into thin strips
1 tablespoon pine nuts, toasted
1 spring onion, white and pale green parts only,
   finely sliced
¼ cup ponzu dressing

Combine all the ingredients in a large salad bowl, tossing well to ensure the dressing thoroughly coats the tuna and salad leaves.

Tuna sashimi and mesclun salad
with ponzu dressing

BLUE-EYE RED CURRY

Serves 2

My real McCoy Malaysian mate Billy reckons my curries are too sweet and not hot enough. The beauty of a recipe like this is that you can make it as sweet or as hot as you want, by throwing in as many sliced chillies as you can cop and a bit more or less palm sugar. It's all about balance and what works for your palate.

400 g blue-eye, bones removed,
    cut into 2 cm pieces
2 tablespoons neutral oil (see page 6)
3 red shallots, finely chopped
2 cloves garlic, crushed
1 knob ginger (about 3 cm long), grated
½ red chilli, sliced (optional)
2 tablespoons ready-made red curry paste
1 tablespoon grated palm sugar
1 tablespoon fish sauce
½ teaspoon salt
200–300 ml coconut milk
200 g bamboo shoots, sliced
steamed rice and steamed Asian greens, to serve

MARINADE
2 tablespoons ready-made red curry paste
1 teaspoon sugar
1 teaspoon fish sauce

Mix the marinade ingredients together in a shallow dish, add the fish and marinate for 2–4 hours, or you could prepare this in the morning and let it marinate all day.

Heat 1 tablespoon of the oil in a large frying pan and sear the blue-eye on both sides in batches, then set aside.

Add the remaining oil to a large saucepan or wok and soften the shallots, but do not brown them. Add the garlic, ginger and fresh chilli, if using, and cook for a minute or so before adding the curry paste. Cook for a few seconds, then add the sugar, fish sauce, salt and coconut milk. Return the fish to the pan and add the bamboo shoots, then simmer for a few minutes until cooked through (do not boil).

Serve with steamed rice and Asian greens.

 Don't overcook the fish or it will turn to mush; just a couple of minutes' simmering should do.

FENNEL RISOTTO

Serves 2

My old advertising and wine-quaffing pal Greg Alder taught me this one about a lifetime ago. It was the first risotto I ever cooked, and it's been a school-night staple for over 25 years at my place (my God, I'm old). You can always tart it up for a dinner party by using homemade stock and adding some pan-fried king prawns.

1 bulb fennel, cored, trimmed and finely diced
2 tablespoons butter
⅔ cup arborio, vialone or carnaroli rice
1 cup ready-made chicken stock (it's a school
**   night, after all), diluted with 1 cup water**
2 tablespoons Pernod
1 tablespoon finely chopped flat-leaf parsley
2 tablespoons freshly grated parmesan cheese

In a large, heavy-based saucepan, soften the fennel in 1 tablespoon of the butter. Add the rice and stir through so the rice is well coated, and cook for a minute or so. Add 1 cup of stock and simmer, while stirring the stock through the rice. Keep adding more stock as the rice absorbs it, a little at a time, for 16–18 minutes. Pour in the Pernod and heat through for a minute or so, then remove the pan from the heat and stir through the parsley, the remaining butter and the parmesan cheese. The final result should be wet and soupy, not too firm – add a little extra stock or water if necessary.

 Fennel is best in winter, so save this dish for the colder months. Having the Pernod out is a good excuse to indulge in a pastis before dinner.

TRIFLE

Serves 6

I am normally stupidly obsessive about the provenance of produce and avoiding processed foods, except when it comes to trifle. Sure, you could make your own sponge, only to ruin the texture by pouring booze all over it. You could make your own custard, but it's trifle, and it's for a school night. So let's all relax and just enjoy this for what it is – a quick and tasty treat at the end of a hard day, with some leftover for tomorrow (yippee).

1 punnet strawberries, sliced
⅓ cup Grand Marnier
1 ready-made sponge cake
2 cups thick ready-made custard
2 cups cream, whipped
2 tablespoons grated dark chocolate
¼ cup flaked almonds, lightly toasted

Marinate the sliced strawberries in 2 tablespoons of the Grand Marnier for 30 minutes.

Cut the sponge into 2 cm cubes and place in the bottom of a glass bowl. Mix the remaining 2 tablespoons of Grand Marnier with an equal amount of water and spoon over the sponge. Top the sponge with half the soaked strawberries.

Spread the custard over the strawberries and top with the remaining strawberries. Cover with whipped cream, then sprinkle over the grated chocolate and flaked almonds. Refrigerate for 1 hour before serving.

 Trifle can have just about anything you want in it: jelly, any sort of fruit or berries, different cakes and whatever booze you fancy (no boys, not VB).

Kids' cooking

Kids' cooking

Life is full of chapters, and I never thought seriously about cooking for kids until I had my daughter, Zoe. Her first solid food was beef congee at a Chinese restaurant, for which I was roundly abused by my wife, although Zoe loved it (she was twelve weeks old). No baby food in jars for her – I cooked her vegetable purées before moving on to tiny slices of pan-fried eye fillet of beef, lamb cutlets, John Dory or salmon. Aged about eight months, she would even toothlessly gum grilled octopus into oblivion.

Zoe was brought up in restaurants, and has always behaved herself in them because of it. We viewed Sunday nights in the highchair at our favourite Chinese restaurant as an investment in the future, as well as a night off cooking. When she was seven, we took her to Paris, and while EuroDisney was the highlight, she behaved wonderfully at the swish Atelier Robuchon, and ate the equivalent of a week's pay at Kaviar Kaspia. While I don't want to turn kids into food snobs, it is nice if their repertoire extends beyond chicken nuggets and fish fingers.

These days it's tough to get kids to eat healthy tucker when their palates are so conditioned by the sweet and salty flavours of processed foods. Sweet treats are fine for special occasions, but we also need to encourage our kids to appreciate real, home-cooked food with fresh meat, fish and vegetables. Here's a selection of recipes featuring real food that kids will love, and they can even get involved in the cooking too – while teaching kids to cook can sometimes be frustrating, it's nearly always a heap of fun. It's also a sure way to make leaving home a more realistic option for them – for more on this, refer back to Chapter 1.

'While teaching kids to cook can sometimes be frustrating, it's nearly always a heap of fun.'

HOMEMADE GNOCCHI WITH TOMATO SAUCE

Serves a small army

Gnocchi is great fun for kids to make, and so very simple. They love the mixing and rolling involved, as well as watching the little balls of potato and flour floating up to the surface when they're cooked.

1 kg desiree or other waxy potatoes
200 g plain flour
½ teaspoon sea salt
1 organic or free-range egg

TOMATO SAUCE
1 large brown onion, very finely chopped
2 cloves garlic, finely sliced or crushed
½ stalk celery, finely chopped
2 tablespoons olive oil
2 tablespoons tomato paste
2 × 400 g can crushed or diced tomatoes
2 tablespoons finely shredded basil
2 tablespoons finely chopped flat-leaf parsley

To make the sauce, soften the onion, garlic and celery in the oil, then stir through the tomato paste and the tomatoes. Bring to a boil then simmer over low heat for 1 hour, adding a little water if it looks like drying out.

Meanwhile, to make the gnocchi, peel and steam or boil the spuds until soft, then drain well and mash. Put a large pan of salted water on to boil. On a clean work surface, mix the mashed potato with the flour, then break the egg into the mix and work in with your fingers. Knead the mixture well until all the ingredients are incorporated. Roll into cylinders about the diameter of a 10 cent piece, then cut into slices 1 cm thick and gently press with a fork to make grooves. Cook in batches in the boiling water (about a dozen at a time – don't overcrowd the pan). The gnocchi are cooked when they rise to the surface.

Stir the basil and parsley through the sauce just before serving and spoon over the just-cooked gnocchi.

CHICKEN SAN CHOY BAU

Serves 4

Kids love anything they can eat with their hands, and san choy bau is no exception. You could take the more traditional route and substitute pork mince for the chicken, as my friend Mathew Chan from Sydney's 33-year-old Peacock Gardens restaurant does. Mathew introduced this dish to Australia, and reckons the restaurant has now served over 250,000 of these pork-filled lettuce leaves.

You'll find lup cheong sausage at Asian butchers or delis.

1 iceberg lettuce (you'll need 8 large leaves in total)
2 tablespoons neutral oil (see page 6)
1 clove garlic, crushed
1 knob ginger (about 3 cm), cut into fine strips
400 g minced chicken
1 lup cheong (Chinese dried sausage), finely sliced
½ cup water chestnuts, roughly chopped or sliced
½ cup bamboo shoots, finely chopped
4 fresh shiitake mushrooms, finely chopped
2 tablespoons hoisin sauce
½ teaspoon rice vinegar

To separate the lettuce leaves from the core without tearing them, trim a slice off the base of the lettuce, and place the lettuce cut-side down under cold running water. The weight of the water will force the leaves apart. Separate eight leaves from the lettuce.

Heat the oil in a wok until very hot, then add the garlic, ginger, mince and lup cheong and stir-fry for a few minutes. Add the water chestnuts, bamboo shoots, mushrooms, hoisin sauce and rice vinegar, and simmer for a minute or two until the meat is cooked through.

Leave the mixture to cool slightly then spoon into the lettuce leaves and serve.

WINTER VEGETABLE SOUP

Serves 6

This is a great way to get kids to eat vegetables. It's a good idea to make a big batch and leave the leftovers in the fridge to have all week (my daughter Zoe loves a cold bowl of this straight after school, and it's significantly better for her than a packet of chips).

25 g butter *or* 2 tablespoons olive oil
1 brown onion, diced
3 carrots, finely sliced
3–4 small zucchini, finely sliced
1 large desiree or other waxy potato, diced
2 cups Homemade Chicken Stock (see page 208) or water
½ cup flat-leaf parsley leaves
½ cup cream (optional)
1 bunch chives, very finely sliced

Heat the oil or butter in a large saucepan and add the onion, carrot, zucchini and potato. Cook for a minute or two, taking care not to let them brown. Pour in the chicken stock and scatter over the parsley. Simmer on low heat until the vegetables are soft.

Purée the soup in a food processor or using a stab blender, then reheat, stirring in the cream, if using. Ladle into bowls, top with the chives and serve.

SPAG BOL WITH LOTS OF VEGGIES

Serves 4–6

OK, so authentic spag bol shouldn't have carrot anywhere near it, and was traditionally cooked with milk, but kids don't know that. They love this version, and it's a great way to sneak a few veggies past the keeper without them noticing. And don't worry – the wine is well and truly cooked out after two hours.

2 tablespoons olive oil
1 kg beef, pork or veal mince
1 large onion, chopped
2 cloves garlic, finely sliced
2 stalks celery, sliced
2 carrots, sliced
2 × 400 g cans diced tomatoes
1 piece orange peel, about 2 cm × 4 cm,
   white pith removed
1 bay leaf
2 tablespoons chopped flat-leaf parsley
1 tablespoon chopped rosemary
1 tablespoon tomato paste (optional)
1 cup dry white wine
sea salt and freshly ground black pepper
400 g spaghetti or the kids' favourite dried pasta
freshly grated parmesan cheese, to serve

Heat the oil in a large saucepan and add the meat, browning well. Add the onion, garlic, celery and carrot and cook for about 5 minutes, until soft. Throw in all the remaining ingredients except the pasta and cheese, add just enough water to cover, and season with salt and pepper. Bring to the boil, then reduce the heat to the gentlest simmer. Place the lid on and cook for 1½–2 hours.

Bring a large saucepan of salted water to a boil, slide in the pasta and cook until al dente.

Serve the pasta with the sauce generously spooned over and top with grated parmesan.

RICE PAPER ROLLS WITH PEANUT SAUCE

Makes 12 rolls

These are great fun to make with the kids, and you can have competitions for the neatest correct entry. Leave the chilli paste out if the kids are in a dipping mood and serve it separately, or make two batches of sauce.

If you have access to a Chinatown or an Asian deli, you could substitute the pork belly for the same amount of Chinese roast pork – this means less time spent cooking, and more time eating.

1 × 150 g piece pork belly
6 fresh, cooked king prawns
1 carrot, coarsely grated, soaked in water with
    a teaspoon of sugar added for a couple of minutes
1 handful fresh bean sprouts
small red oak or mignonette lettuce,
    soft outer and middle leaves only, washed
1 bunch garlic or regular chives
12 mint leaves
12 round sheets rice paper
about 75 g rice vermicelli

PEANUT SAUCE
2 large cloves garlic, crushed
1 teaspoon neutral oil (see page 6)
2 tablespoons tomato paste
1 teaspoon chilli paste
1 teaspoon sugar
2 tablespoons peanut butter
2 tablespoons hoisin sauce
2 tablespoons roasted peanuts, ground

Preheat the oven to 180°C and roast the pork belly for 1 hour. When cool enough to handle, cut into thin slices.

To make the sauce, fry the garlic in the oil in a small frying pan until soft. Add the tomato and chilli pastes and cook for a few seconds, then add the sugar, peanut butter, hoisin sauce and ⅓ cup water and stir to combine. Simmer gently for a couple of minutes, then remove from the heat and set aside to cool to room temperature.

Peel the prawns and lay them on a cutting board. With a sharp knife, cut them all the way through from head to tail lengthways, so you have two thin, flat halves.

Arrange all the prepared vegetables in bowls in front of you, so you can just scoop out what you need easily.

Soak the vermicelli in warm water for a few minutes until soft, and drain immediately before using.

Soak the rice paper sheets, one or two at a time, in a large bowl of warm water for about a minute, then transfer to a clean tea towel.

Take a sheet of rice paper and arrange a piece of prawn, a slice of pork, some vermicelli, carrot, bean shoots, lettuce, chives and mint in the bottom left-hand corner, then roll a couple of times, fold it in half, and roll again. Repeat until all the rolls are filled, placing them on a plate and covering them with a damp tea towel as you go, and serve straightaway with the sauce.

FRIED RICE

Serves 4–6

This is a classic family meal and, in my experience, there is something irresistible about using an omelette as an ingredient – half of it usually disappears along the way. You could trick this up with all sorts of fancy ingredients, but I reckon fried rice is too sacred to mess with. In Australian culinary history, it's right up there next to a hamburger with beetroot.

2 organic or free-range eggs
¼ cup neutral oil (see page 6)
2 cups long-grain rice
2 spring onions, finely sliced
⅔ cup small frozen cooked prawns, thawed
½ cup frozen peas
1 small piece char siu (Chinese barbecued pork),
    finely chopped
2 tablespoons light soy sauce
1 teaspoon sea salt
½ teaspoon sesame oil (optional)

Beat the eggs together in a small bowl. Heat 1 tablespoon of the oil in a non-stick frying pan, pour in the eggs and cook until set in the middle. Leave to cool slightly, chop the omelette into small pieces and set aside.

Bring plenty of salted water to a boil in a large saucepan, then add the rice and simmer, uncovered, for about 10 minutes, or until the rice is cooked. Rinse under cold water, drain and set aside.

Heat the remaining oil in a large wok and lightly cook the spring onion, then add the prawns, peas and char siu, stirring briefly. Add the omelette pieces and rice, breaking up any clumps with your wooden spoon. Cook for a minute or two, then stir through the soy sauce, salt and the sesame oil, if using, and serve.

CHINTA RIA'S FRIED CHICKEN

Serves 4

When my wife and I lived in Melbourne nearly twenty years ago, we ate this chicken dish almost every week at jazz-lover Simon Goh's restaurant, Chinta Ria. The recipe later featured in a wonderful book called *Hot Food, Cool Jazz*, which Simon co-wrote with foodies Terry Durack and Jill Dupleix in the 1990s. The original uses chicken legs, but I use thigh fillets as I find they cook faster and more evenly. There are no flavours in here too challenging for school-aged kids.

6 chicken thigh fillets, whole or cut into
    bite-sized pieces
about 1 cup neutral oil (see page 6), for cooking
1 lemon, cut into quarters
steamed rice and steamed Asian greens, to serve

MARINADE
1 tablespoon Malay curry powder
1 teaspoon turmeric
1 teaspoon five-spice powder
1 organic or free-range egg, beaten
1 teaspoon sugar
½ teaspoon sea salt
½ tablespoon oyster sauce
½ tablespoon soy sauce
1 tablespoon cornflour
1 teaspoon Chinese rice wine *or* dry sherry
1 teaspoon sesame oil

Mix all the marinade ingredients together in a large shallow dish. Add the chicken and marinate in the fridge for 12–24 hours.

Heat a 1 cm-layer of oil in a frying pan and fry the chicken until golden brown and cooked through, turning once. Remove from the pan and drain on kitchen paper. Squeeze the lemon juice over, and serve with steamed rice and Asian greens.

 If you can face messing about with raw chicken in the morning, throw the marinade together before work, leave the chicken to marinade in it while you're out, and the hard yakka is already done.

CHICKEN AND SWEETCORN SOUP

Serves 4

When cooking this for kids, the temptation is to try to get it to taste like Chinese takeaway. Don't bother – you'd have to add obscene amounts of salt and sugar, which makes you worry just how much rubbish is in the average takeaway dinner. The amounts I've included here are plenty – and it tastes delicious.

4 cups Homemade Chicken Stock (see page 208)
⅓ cup creamed corn
1 teaspoon sugar
½ teaspoon sea salt
1 cup finely diced cooked chicken fillet
1 tablespoon cornflour, dissolved in
  2 tablespoons water
1 large or 2 small organic or free-range eggs,
  lightly beaten

Heat the chicken stock in a wok or large saucepan until boiling. Add the corn, sugar, salt, chicken and the cornflour mixture. Turn the heat to low and cook for about a minute until the soup thickens, then stir through the beaten egg, and serve immediately.

REAL CHICKEN NOODLE SOUP

Serves 4

Forget about canned soup – there is nothing quite like making chicken noodle soup with fresh chicken for your kids. The flavours are so clean and simple; you can almost feel it doing them good.

If you are smart enough to have some homemade chicken stock in the freezer, then this is a 5 minute dinner – just defrost the stock and reheat it with the noodles added (skip the chicken breast, or add some skinless barbecued chicken meat). Otherwise, this is great for a Sunday-night special, when you'll have all afternoon to cook your stock.

6 cups Homemade Chicken Stock (see page 208)
1 cup dried egg noodles, broken into 1–2 cm pieces
sea salt and freshly ground black pepper
½ cooked chicken breast fillet, finely sliced
1 tablespoon chopped flat-leaf parsley or chives

Bring the stock to a boil in a large saucepan. Add the noodles and reduce the heat to low, simmering for 5–10 minutes until the noodles are cooked. Season to taste with salt and pepper.

Place the chicken slices, along with the fresh parsley or chives, in the bottom of four serving bowls. Ladle the soup over and serve.

SPAGHETTI WITH FOUR CHEESES

Serves 4

The classic spaghetti *quattro formaggi* is a bit of a grown-up twist on macaroni cheese, but a lot of kids I know love its slurpy, creamy richness. If you think the flavours might be too strong for kids, you can replace the pecorino cheese with cheddar.

400 g spaghetti or penne
¼ cup milk
¼ cup pouring cream
30 g fontina cheese, diced
30 g parmesan cheese, freshly grated
30 g pecorino cheese, freshly grated
30 g gruyère cheese, freshly grated
½ teaspoon nutmeg
½ teaspoon finely chopped rosemary
½ teaspoon finely chopped oregano
1 teaspoon finely chopped parsley
1 egg yolk

Bring a large saucepan of water to the boil, slide in the pasta and cook until al dente.

Meanwhile, in a medium-sized non-stick frying pan add the milk, cream, cheeses and nutmeg and cook over low heat, stirring with a wooden spoon. When the cheese has melted, stir through the herbs and remove the pan from the heat.

Place the egg yolk in a small cup and add about 5 tablespoons of the sauce, stirring well so the egg doesn't scramble (the heat of the sauce will cook the egg). Add the drained pasta to the cheese mixture, stirring through to coat the pasta completely. Stir through the egg mixture and serve immediately.

CHANG'S ROCKY ROAD

Makes plenty

You won't find this recipe on the menu at fine-dining restaurants, but six-year-olds don't care. Initially developed as a joke while coming up with recipes for a friend's Asian foods business, Zoe and her school friends didn't think it was funny – just scrumptious – and we have had fried noodles in our rocky road ever since.

250 g milk chocolate
1 cup white marshmallows, cut into pieces
½ cup leftover red jelly *or* ½ cup soft jelly/jube lollies, cut into pieces
⅔ × 100 g pack Chang's Original Fried Noodles, available from supermarkets

Line a plastic takeaway container or other micro-waveable container with a piece of greaseproof paper.

Break the chocolate into pieces, place in the container and microwave for 2 minutes or until just melted. Stir through the marshmallows, jelly or lollies and the fried noodles, and place in the fridge until the chocolate hardens.

Remove from the container, peel off the greaseproof paper, and cut into pieces about 2 cm square.

KOULORIA
Makes plenty

Here is the only Greek culinary trapping that I possess. My mum (who's not Greek at all) made these all through my childhood, although they always tasted better when made by my Greek relatives on my dad's side (sorry, Mum).

Making these involves rolling lots of long, skinny snakes and the chance to get plenty of flour all over everybody.

250 g butter, softened
1 cup caster sugar
4 organic or free-range eggs
1 egg white, lightly beaten
1 kg self-raising flour, with 1 tablespoon cinnamon
    and ½ teaspoon salt mixed through
½–¾ cup milk, mixed with 2 teaspoons vanilla extract
½ cup sesame seeds

Preheat the oven to 180°C. Blend the butter in a food processor until soft and creamy. Add the sugar and mix until incorporated, then add the eggs, one at a time, mixing so that each one is incorporated before adding the next. Add the flour mixture and milk mixture alternately, a little at a time, and process until incorporated.

Take a handful of the mixture and roll it into a cylinder about 16 cm long and the thickness of a pencil. Fold in half and twist the two lengths together to form a plait. Repeat with the rest of the mixture.

Brush the biscuits with the beaten egg white and sprinkle with sesame seeds. Place the biscuits on a baking tray lined with greaseproof paper, and cook for 20–25 minutes, until golden brown. Cool on racks and store in airtight containers.

TOASTED CHOCOLATE AND MARSHMALLOW SANDWICHES

Serves 4–8

These are sugary-sweet and, unsurprisingly, kids love them. But they also make very nice sweet treats to have with coffee and a liqueur muscat or cognac after the little darlings have gone to bed.

butter, for spreading
8 × 1 cm-thick slices brioche loaf
100 g good quality dark chocolate, coarsely grated
1 cup white marshmallows, sliced

Lightly butter the brioche slices on one side. Take one slice and, on the unbuttered side, arrange a thick layer of chocolate and some marshmallow pieces, then top with another slice of brioche, buttered-side out. Repeat with the rest of the sandwiches, then fry them in a dry non-stick frying pan over medium heat so the chocolate and marshmallow melts, turning once. Cut into halves and serve.

 If you can't get brioche, use thick-sliced white bread instead.

WAFFLES

Makes plenty

Even though I have a gadget phobia, a $50 electric waffle iron seems like good value to me if you have the cupboard space. And it'll pay for itself in no time if you have kids – waffle-making is a great way to kill time on a rainy Sunday morning. You could also try these with the caramel sauce on page 72.

2 cups plain flour
1 heaped teaspoon baking powder
1 teaspoon table salt
¼ cup caster sugar
800 ml buttermilk
3 organic or free-range eggs, separated
50 g butter, melted
vanilla ice cream, to serve

CHOCOLATE FUDGE SAUCE
¾ cup thickened cream
100 g dark chocolate (70% cocoa)

Combine all the dry ingredients in a bowl. Add the buttermilk, egg yolks, and then the melted butter, mixing well between each addition to incorporate.

Whisk the egg whites until soft peaks form and fold through the mixture. Ladle into a waffle iron and cook until golden brown.

Meanwhile, to make the sauce, gently warm the cream in a saucepan and add the chocolate, stirring until the chocolate has melted.

Serve the waffles with the warm chocolate sauce and some vanilla ice cream.

My daughter Zoe once put in a rare lunch order at the school canteen, and arrived home distraught. 'They put canned tuna in the sushi,' she complained. The two remarkable things about this were that: 1) they sold any sort of sushi at a school canteen; and 2) Zoe considered herself a sushi expert (she was five years old at the time).

Sushi is everywhere. It's the new cappuccino. It's healthy, it's not expensive and kids love it. Pity then that so much of the sushi whizzing around on the average suburban sushi train is of such low quality. Given that I won't take Zoe to her favourite local Japanese restaurant every night, and she avoids the school-canteen sushi (pasta has a much smaller margin for error), Zoe now has me making sushi at home every other week.

Sushi is simple to master. First and foremost, you'll need a rice cooker. It's not absolutely essential, but it's pretty hard to get sushi rice spot-on without one. You'll also need a sushi mat, some sushi rice, nori (sheets of seaweed) and seasoned rice vinegar (an all-in-one blend that saves you mixing up sugar, salt and vinegar), all of which you can find in some larger supermarkets or Japanese specialty stores. The only real effort lies in buying a small amount of sashimi-grade fish (usually salmon or tuna), this grading being an indicator of absolute quality and freshness. (Sushi, perhaps more than any other food, relies on the best quality produce. You don't want your kids, or anyone else for that matter, eating raw fish that isn't fantastically fresh.)

The other part of the equation is your technique, or in my case, lack of it. Of the two basic types of sushi – nigiri (a slice of fish on rice) and makimono (a rolled-up thingy) – nigiri requires a lot more skill, so my tip would be to start with the rolled-up thingies; they are much more forgiving.

Make your sushi rice just before you are going to serve it, as refrigeration makes the rice grains harden.

If you knew sushi...

SUSHI RICE
Makes enough for 2 rolls

1 cup sushi rice
2 tablespoons seasoned rice vinegar

Rinse the rice with water three times, then place in the rice cooker with 1 cup water and cook until tender (or alternatively, bring 2 cups of water to boil in a saucepan then add the rice, turn the heat to low, and simmer gently with the lid on until the rice is cooked). Turn the cooker off (or remove the pan from the heat) and leave the rice to rest for 20 minutes, covered with a damp tea towel, before gently folding through the seasoned rice vinegar to coat. Allow the rice to cool to body temperature before using – test by sticking a (clean) finger in; it should feel neither hot nor cold.

MAKIMONO
Makes 2 rolls

2 sheets nori
1 quantity cooked sushi rice
150 g sashimi-grade salmon or tuna, cut into 5 mm wide pieces (of course you could use canned tuna, but buy the stuff in water, not olive oil)
½ avocado, peeled and de-seeded, flesh cut into 1 cm thick strips
½ cucumber, peeled and de-seeded, flesh cut into 5 mm thick strips
⅛ iceberg lettuce, cut into fine strips
1 × 250 g bottle Japanese mayonnaise or ½ cup good quality ready-made mayonnaise
Japanese soy sauce and wasabi paste, to serve

Place a sheet of nori shiny-side down on a sushi mat, with the shorter side facing you. Leave the width of two pieces of bamboo between the end of the mat farthest from you and the nori.

Wet your hands and take a handful of rice, placing it on the nori and spreading it out to the edges (but leave a 1 cm gap at the edge farthest from you). The rice should lie on top of the nori in a thick slab, about two or three grains high.

Pile about half the fish, avocado, cucumber and lettuce on the rice at the end nearest to you, leaving a border around the edges so that the filling is not pushed out. Squeeze a generous line of mayo on top of the fish. Pick up the mat at the near-end and roll it up into a square shape. Tap the filling in at both ends with your fingers. (Don't be too discouraged if the filling bursts out of the roll or it all falls apart on you – sushi skills really do improve with practise. My first effort was greeted with 'It tastes pretty good, but it looks terrible, Dad.' I suggest you have a couple of goes before showing off in front of a bunch of picky second-graders.)

Repeat the process with the remaining ingredients to make another roll. Wet the end of a very sharp knife (so the nori doesn't tear), and cut the rolls in half, then slice each half into four or five equal pieces, and serve with Japanese soy sauce and wasabi paste.

The basics

Mastering these basic recipes will add miles of flavour to your everyday cooking. Try them just once and I promise, you'll never want to resort to the ready-made alternatives again.

CLASSIC VINAIGRETTE

There are a million variations on a good salad dressing, but as long you stick to the ratio of 2–3 parts oil to 1 part acidulant, you can't go wrong. You could trick it up with garlic, herbs, or whatever takes your fancy, but it's hard to beat this simple version. Just make sure you use the best oil and vinegar you can afford.

½–¾ **cup olive oil**
¼ **cup acidulant (lemon or lime juice,**
   red-, white-wine or balsamic vinegar)
sea salt and freshly ground black pepper
½ **teaspoon Dijon mustard (optional)**

Mix all the ingredients together.

HOMEMADE CHICKEN STOCK
Makes 2–3 litres

Making your own chicken stock is a breeze and is absolutely the best way to add miles of flavour to savoury dishes. This recipe makes a delicious stock, but for an even simpler version, it's perfectly acceptable just to take a whole chicken, cover it with cold water in a stockpot and simmer for a few hours, à la Neil Perry.

1 whole chook, trimmed of excess fat *or*
   1 kg chicken bones
1 carrot, roughly chopped
1 brown onion, roughly chopped
1 stalk celery, roughly chopped
1 bay leaf
8 whole peppercorns

Place all the ingredients into a stockpot and cover with cold water by 2–3 cm. Bring to the boil then reduce the heat and simmer, uncovered, for 1–1½ hours, skimming any scum from the top now and then.
   Strain the stock through a fine sieve into a container, reserving the cooked chicken meat (which can be used in soups, pies or sandwiches) and discarding the rest of the solids. Cool the stock in the fridge, then remove the solidified fat from the surface. The stock can be stored in the fridge for 2–3 days, or frozen.

HOMEMADE FISH STOCK
Makes 2–3 litres

OK, so this might be a bit smelly and messy to make at home, but it's really hard to find a good ready-made fish stock, so you're better off throwing one together yourself. And if you're cooking a dish that requires fish stock (like a chowder, fish soup or seafood risotto), you'll be buying seafood anyway, so just ask your fishmonger to throw in some fish bones as well.

head and bones of 1 white fish, washed
½ **carrot, roughly chopped**
1 small brown onion, roughly chopped
½ **stalk celery, roughly chopped**
about 6 whole black peppercorns
about 6 stems parsley (stalks only)

Place all the ingredients into a stockpot and cover with cold water by 2–3 cm. Bring to the boil then reduce the heat and simmer, uncovered, for 20 minutes, skimming any scum from the top now and then.
   Strain the stock through a fine sieve into a container. The stock can be stored in the fridge for 2–3 days, or frozen.

HOMEMADE MAYONNAISE
Makes 1 cup

Don't be intimidated by the thought of making your own mayonnaise: it's much easier than you'd expect. You'll probably need a couple of practice runs to get it right (as well as an assistant to act as oil-drizzler).

2 egg yolks
½ **teaspoon Dijon mustard**
about 1 cup olive oil
sea salt, to taste
lemon juice, to taste

Place the egg yolks and Dijon mustard in a large bowl. Add the olive oil in a fine drizzle while whisking vigorously with a wire whisk or a fork until the mixture thickens. (You can cheat and use an electric mixer if you must.) Season with a little sea salt and add a few drops of lemon juice.

Index

VIKING

Published by the Penguin Group
Penguin Group (Australia)
250 Camberwell Road, Camberwell, Victoria 3124, Australia
(a division of Pearson Australia Group Pty Ltd)
Penguin Group (USA) Inc.
375 Hudson Street, New York, New York 10014, USA
Penguin Group (Canada)
90 Eglinton Avenue East, Suite 700, Toronto, Canada ON M4P 2Y3
(a division of Pearson Penguin Canada Inc.)
Penguin Books Ltd
80 Strand, London WC2R 0RL England
Penguin Ireland
25 St Stephen's Green, Dublin 2, Ireland
(a division of Penguin Books Ltd)
Penguin Books India Pvt Ltd
11 Community Centre, Panchsheel Park, New Delhi – 110 017, India
Penguin Group (NZ)
67 Apollo Drive, Rosedale, North Shore 0632, New Zealand
(a division of Pearson New Zealand Ltd)
Penguin Books (South Africa) (Pty) Ltd
24 Sturdee Avenue, Rosebank, Johannesburg 2196, South Africa

Penguin Books Ltd, Registered Offices: 80 Strand, London, WC2R 0RL, England

First published by Penguin Group (Australia), 2008

10 9 8 7 6 5 4 3 2 1

Text copyright © Kim Terakes 2008
Photographs copyright © Rob Palmer 2008

The moral right of the author has been asserted

Design by Daniel New © Penguin Group (Australia)
Australian Gourmet Traveller photograph on page 3 by Stuart Spence
Styling by Jane Hann
Typeset in Glypha and Univers by Post Pre-press Group, Brisbane, Queensland
Colour reproduction by Splitting Image Colour Studio Pty Ltd, Clayton, Victoria
Printed in China by Everbest Printing Co. Ltd.

National Library of Australia
Cataloguing-in-Publication data:

Terakes, Kim.
The great Aussie bloke's cookbook / Kim Terakes
9780670072484 (pbk.)
Includes index.
Cookery.
Male cooks--Australia.

641.51

penguin.com.au

Acknowledgements

Firstly, my sincere thanks go to Penguin publisher
Julie Gibbs, who took a punt on my first book, *The Great
Aussie Barbie Cookbook*, and backed this one before the
first had established its success.

This book is pretty much my history with food and
therefore a very personal story, and because of this,
I have possibly been even more of a pain in the butt
to deal with than usual, so thanks to all at Penguin for
putting up with me. Virginia Birch edited my words like
someone who is great at what they do – I could rarely
tell what she had changed. Daniel New did a top job with
the design, making the recipes easy to follow and the
whole book so user-friendly. Ingrid Ohlsson ran the show
(and me) with her usual professional aplomb. All three
of them also prevented this book for blokes looking and
reading like a copy of *Penthouse*, which was probably
my natural inclination.

The lovely, and definitely un-blokey, Jane Hann did
a wonderful job styling the shots and coping with the
very un-lovely me. And photographer Rob Palmer made
the hard stuff look easy, shooting more than we should
each day, pulling me into line where necessary, and
generally being so relaxed and laid-back to work with
while delivering a great result.

This book wouldn't exist at all if not for the Boys Can
Cook classes. My thanks to all those who have come
along for a laugh, especially regulars like Nick, Sonia,
Tom, Adele and Booker. Blanco have been the most
generous hosts for three years and provide the perfect
environment for the classes. Richard Morgan from
Morganware, Cantarella Bros. and The Essential
Ingredient have supplied their fabulous products, and,
week in, week out, Steve Costi Seafoods, Fratelli Fresh
and AC Butchery provide produce that is simply a joy to
cook with. My thanks go to Steve Costi and Rob from the
city store, Fratelli's Barry and Jamie McDonald, Carlo and
Arnaldo Colaiacomo from AC, and Ben and Kate from
their Rose Bay outlet. All these people have helped me
help blokes (and many girls) who hadn't cooked before
discover how much fun it can be, and how rewarding it
is to share good food. I've had a ball doing it.